HAUNTED MADISON COUNTY

Rebecca Patrick-Howard

With

Suzie Ratliff & Peter Howard

Haunted Madison County

Copyright © 2015 by Rebecca Patrick-Howard

www.rebeccaphoward.net

Published by Mistletoe Press

All rights reserved. No part of this book may be reproduced, scanned, or distributed in any printed or electronic form without permission.

First Edition: November 2015

Printed in the United States of America

For Kristy, Suzie, Bobby Sue, JR, Chris, Brian, David, Bonnie, and the rest of us who used to know the county roads like the backs of our hands…

TABLE OF CONTENTS

Haunted Madison County 1

Table of Contents 4

Introduction 1

Westover Terrace 7

    Janet's Story 17

    Jerry's Story 19

    My Story 21

    Suzie's Story 23

White Hall 28

    Lindsey's Story 34

    My Story 36

    Claire's Story 38

Waco Tales 42

    The Moberly Hanging Man 44

    Jason's Story 45

    The Waco Spy 48

    Sweet Miss Sarah 50

    The Elliston Farm House..54

The Cane Patch Murder..57

    Dana's Story...60

    Dolores' Story 62

The Glyndon Hotel..68

A Fun Night at the Opera 70

Little Egypt 72

    The Hauntings 73

    Lois, Julia, and Little Egypt.......................................74

    Chris' Story...76

    Dylan's Story..78

    Who WAS Little Egypt? 80

The Pigg House 83

    J.D.'s Story..86

    More Pigg Stories... 88

Madison Middle School 90

    Sherry's Story..92

A Rental Horror..95

The Richmond Kangaroo 100

    Erin's Kangaroo Story 101

Why a Kangaroo?..104

Black Helicopters..106

Random Richmond Stories....................................110

    A Murder and a Hanging 111

    UFO Blitz 113

    The Lizard Creature..116

    Haunted Cholera Graves 118

    Elmwood...119

The Tunnels..121

EKU Ghosts...126

    Burnam Hall...126

    Keene Hall..129

    The Restrooms..131

    Moore Building 132

    Mozart, the Dog...133

    Alumni House 134

Sullivan Hall...135

    Emily's Story 137

    Carol's Story 139

Clay Hall..142

Pearl Buchanan Theatre 146

    Amanda's Story 148

    J.D.'s Story 150

    Who IS the Blue Lady? 152

Boone Tavern 154

Berea Tales 157

    Moran Summit Road 159

    Jefferson Street Railroad Crossing 161

    Flat Gap Church 162

    US 25 House 163

    The Cowbell Cemetery 164

    Conspiracy Theory 165

    The "Cow" Story 166

    Berea College 167

Other Haunted Houses 172

    Barnes Mill Road 174

    Locust Avenue 176

    Westover Avenue 177

    Mount Vernon Road 180

    The Breck House 181

Slave Houses	182
Salem Cemetery	184
The Gypsy Death	186
Lillian Bains Karnes	188
Additional Photos	191
Special Thanks	195
References	197
About the Author	204
Let's Connect!	206
A Broom with a View	207
Other Books	210

INTRODUCTION

ARE GHOST STORIES important? Do they mean anything? Are they necessary?

The fact is, folklore has always been an integral part of not only Appalachian culture but as far back as recorded history can remember. Who were the Greeks and Romans without their mythology? What would we know of the Celts without their stories? Long before television, telephones, and the Internet, oral history was how we spread the news: stories were passed on, and the culture and identity of a place were shaped.

Of course, by today's standards, some of the older stories sound outlandish and improbable, but they weren't always meant to be taken at face value. Often, stories and urban legends, and especially fairy tales, carried morals with them–morals that served as important life lessons, warnings, and instructions for that time. They reflected an area's culture, time period, and even current events. Morality tales were frequently told to warn young people from going astray. Look at the story of the young couple parked on Lover's

Lane, who get attacked by a man with a hook (or an escaped mental facility patient or a man with an ax...the story changes a lot). That particular story was popularized in the 1950s when teenagers were beginning to date (as opposed to socializing in group settings) and, more importantly, it was when the "family car" became a more prominent structure in dating. So what was the moral of that story? Don't go parking alone with your girlfriend or else you might get killed.

Then there were family tales, stories either re-told or even just created to share the history of one's lineage (be them true or not).

And, of course, the "scary stories" were often simply used for entertainment purposes. That has never been out of style and will hopefully (for some of us anyway) never will be).

It might sound funny today, but "creepy" stories as we know them now were used as entertainment during Christmas gatherings rather than for the Halloween scares we see in slasher films today. We hear a lot about the "old-fashioned Christmas" and how the season used to be a time for gathering the family and creating one's form of entertainment. However, that sometimes included trying to outdo one another with horror stories about ogres and demons and witches and other chilling tales that are now more recognized with Halloween. (Okay, in some of our families we might still do that at Christmas...)

I grew up in Madison County. I have a strong sense of familiarity with a lot of places I've written about in this book.

For many, many years I lived on Eastern Kentucky University's campus in one of the dorms (Telford) where my mother was area coordinator. My mother also worked in the library at Berea College, and we lived in university housing just three doors down from Boone Tavern.

During my teenage years, I lived near Curtis Pike and used to ride my bike (sometimes in the middle of the night with a flashlight for "headlights" to Lake Wilgreen). And, for a short time, I lived in Richmond Manor Apartments while my mother was a college student. In fact, many of the friends I still have more than thirty years later are those I met during my residency at Richmond Manor–many of us living there and playing together while our parents sought higher education or better jobs. It was a wonderful time in my life.

So I have lived all over Madison County, although I now make my home in Irvine (though my mom lives in Waco).

As teenagers without any money, my friends and I used to pull our money for gas (back when we could fill up for less than $15), turn the radio up, and drive around "exploring" as we'd try to find the specters that haunted the various mysterious places around the county. We visited Salem Cemetery, Little Egypt, Westover Terrace, the Pigg House, Eastern's dorms...

Not long ago, I was in a local business, and the cashier asked me about this book and inquired about its release date. We began talking about some of the ghost stories, and I mentioned the Cane Patch Murder and asked if she'd heard of it, or heard of the ghost of the headless woman associated with the story. She hadn't. I told her that many people had told me a variation of that tale, but that the stories had come from an older generation.

"That's why I'm glad you're doing this," she replied. "So that the future generations remember these when the rest of us are gone."

Incidentally, that's why I began collecting these stories in the first place–for my kids to enjoy them one day.

I gathered the following stories through research, online and off. Some of them are from my own personal experiences. Several people submitted stories to me on my website. If they wanted credit, I kept their real names. Many wanted to be anonymous. I noted that where applicable.

Some asked that I edit and proofread their stories. Others didn't mind if I left them as-is. These are denoted as well.

Some readers might read through the book and wonder why I didn't mention Haunted Location A or Haunted Location B. The fact is, I could probably write a whole other book about additional locations here in the county. I am still getting stories sent to me and to my editor. I wanted to use authentic experiences from real people here in the county, and not make anything up. So I worked with what I had at the time.

Of course, now I have more. That's how I ended up with two volumes of *Haunted Estill County*.

A good friend of mine, fellow local author Keven McQueen, wrote the following on his website:

The bloated, headless corpse of a woman; a disembodied head resting atop a mound; a bloody corn knife; a ghost car. All of these elements combined to give Madison Countians bad dreams in 1936. (http://www.kevenmcqueenstories.com/published_works)

You'll find mentions of those and more in the ensuing pages...

(And then you might want to check out some of Keven's books, too!)

I hope the following book brings back some fond memories for those of you who, like my friends and I, also explored the backroads and countryside on those dark nights, the winding roads before they became subdivisions and bypasses.

And I hope that on some late, quiet night when you're up reading alone, it may even bring a few goosebumps.

WESTOVER TERRACE

EVERY TOWN HAS that one house—the uninhabited place that's old enough to have a history yet mysterious enough so that most people don't know what that history may be. And, of course, a house that's beautiful and unique enough so that no other house in town looks like it.

Enter Westover Terrace.

Westover Terrace has been empty for the majority of my lifetime (we won't talk numbers but, suffice to say, we're talking multiple decades here). With a location on one of the most beautiful lots in town, its sprawling lawn looks like a park, full of towering trees, a ravine, and a winding driveway. When the leaves are on the trees, passersby might not even notice it; the only visible aspects are the slanting red roofs that look like something from a Mediterranean country.

Upon closer inspection, architect and history buffs alike are struck by the striking front porch that wraps around the front and accessed via a winding staircase that's an entire story tall. The "carriage porch" is one of the house's most striking features, although it's not the only unique feature—even without counting the ghosts.

There are two round rooms (the top one is known as "pyramidal") within the house, one above the other, and the stained glass windows throw a spattering of colorful patterns on the old wooden floors inside.

The house, originally known as the "Wilkes Smith" house, is a combination of Queen Anne and Shingles style architecture. The Queen Anne style can certainly be seen in the house's asymmetry and delicate details around the terrace, although it also has a certain Italianate feel to it as well.

The house has seen many owners over the years including Dr. A Wilkes Smith, who was a local dentist, and the house's first owner. It gained notoriety, too, as being the home of Elise Bennett, Cassius Clay's granddaughter. (Don't worry, we'll get to the Clay family in a little while!) Local business owner, Graham Nichols, and his wife own the house now.

Not all of Westover's owners resided in the house. For instance, a local funeral home owned it for awhile, purportedly buying it with the intentions of turning it into a business. Alas, these plans never manifested for multiple reasons and, as a result, the house remained empty for many years.

It later sold to the Nichols, who bought it with plans of restoring the beautiful home to its former glory. They WERE (thankfully for those of us who love old houses and history) able to restore it and now live in the house, giving it life again for the first time in many years.

I've had the pleasure of touring the house on many occasions. Before the funeral home owned it, I became friends with the caretaker who lived around the corner. At that time, the house had its original fireplace mantles and banister (these were later either stolen or sold at auction, depending on who you ask). It was also full of furniture–some of which had been there for many, many years. In fact, I remember those first few visits feeling as though I was traversing a darkened labyrinth, the obstacles random pieces of furniture and debris that littered the floors. I have since toured it with Graham himself, back when he was still in the beginning phases of remodeling it. Graham and his wife introduced themselves via my website, which they found while doing research on their new home.

I was only twelve years old on my first walk-through of the house but was still taken aback by its beauty. Even though the rooms were dark and cluttered and difficult to maneuver, and I'd heard horror stories about the house and its many ghosts, I felt nothing unusual. Still, I became a bit obsessed with it and began visiting the local library to research everything from its history to architectural details.

Later, as a teenager, some friends and I received permission from the owner to visit the house and photograph it. It was on these trips that I took the majority of the pictures I now have. We would spend hours there, walking slowly through the rooms and photographing the tiniest of details, all taken by different aspects we fell in love with.

Although, at that time, the house was empty and we heard of other teenagers going there to vandalize and otherwise disturb the house, we never had those intentions. In fact, we often took a broom in an attempt to clear out the many leaves and much debris that blew in from the outside. Unfortunately, thanks to those who did have less than stellar intentions where the house was concerned, we were eventually told not to return, our invitation to the house discontinued.

I remember leaving in tears that day, feeling like someone had kicked me out of my own home.

These days, the house has a reputation for being one of the most haunted houses in Richmond and can be found on several "haunted places" websites. It also has other rumors associated with it.

For instance, some believe that an underground tunnel exists, connecting the cellar to Four Mile Road. (I have lived in Madison County for most of my life and had never heard of this until I read someone's entry on Virtual Tourist, nor had previous owners, or members of the Historical Society I spoke to, heard this rumor.)

The idea is barely probable, not to mention a confusing theory since such a tunnel would have served no real purpose. I've spent quite a bit of time in the house's cellar and have seen no signs of a doorway. Also, the "tunnel" would have to stretch on for more than a mile and go through at least one water source. (Not to mention the fact that there is no reason such a tunnel would even exist.)

Still, the house does hold quite a bit of history that can still be found on the walls and in the ground–quite literally.

I remember seeing old recipes written on the walls when I used to explore the house. According to an article in the Richmond Register, the current owners are also aware of the recipes, one of which was for poison, and covered them with acrylic to preserve them for posterity.

Bullet casings, presumably left over from the Civil War, have been found on the lawn. There are also signs that the grounds (which were once larger but were sectioned off for new housing developments several years ago) were used as a graveyard at one time.

So who haunts the ghosts of Westover Terrace?

Graham Nichols, the current owner, has had his own experience with the ghosts of his house. According to the Richmond Register, he was at the house alone, working on the windows and doors, when he heard "what sounded like a sledge hammer strike an old stove that was behind the wall" where he was standing. A few minutes later it sounded like someone was moving the stove across the room. Graham admitted that he "just dropped all [his] tools and took off running" (Richmond Register, King, 2015).

The Nichols also experienced other strange occurrences while attempting to renovate Westover. Whenever they or their contractors worked on the house, they'd heard banging and crashing sounds that were apparently not part of the renovations. In fact, some of the contractors quit, thanks to the other ghostly workers. Graham described one common sound as being like "a spring being wound up followed by a large gust of wind inside the house" that was comparable only to the noise you might get if you "[stood] on the interstate and [were] passed by a large truck."

The Nichols aren't the only ones to have supernatural experiences with the house, however…

JANET'S STORY

The following story was sent to me by "Janet", a local woman, who submitted her tale via my author website.

"Janet," moved to Richmond as a teenager in the 1990s, spent quite a bit of time in the house with her boyfriend when both were in high school. She says that on one occasion, late at night, she and her boyfriend were in one of the downstairs bedrooms when both were shaken by the sound of a woman upstairs, "crying her eyes out." At first, Janet's boyfriend was convinced that another couple was in the house and had simply been arguing. But then, both heard the sound of frantic footsteps as someone ran from one room to another above them. Thinking there might be trouble, Janet's boyfriend went upstairs to check, a flashlight in his hand.

There wasn't anyone there.

Jimmy, another local man, worked at the house off and on during the 1980s. One day he said he was outside, doing some work on the grounds when he got the feeling someone was watching him. When he looked up, he saw a man peering out from one of the upstairs windows. Jimmy knew there shouldn't be anyone else in the house and was afraid that someone had broken in.

Jimmy put down his tools and went up to the second floor. There was only one exit to the house at the time, and nobody could have reached it without passing by him. He searched throughout the house but couldn't find any signs of anyone having been inside.

JERRY'S STORY

Another Richmond native, "Jerry", had a similar experience when he was a teenager and visiting the house with friends.

Jerry, sixteen years old at the time and his friends drove out to the house after dark one Saturday night. They'd heard many ghost stories about the place and wanted to check it out for themselves.

There were five of them, and they went through all the rooms, sticking close together. The others were laughing and cutting up, but Jerry was in a hurry to get out. He felt like there was something in the house that didn't want them there so he kept ushering the others through the rooms as quickly as he could, hoping to hurry them along.

When they returned to the first floor and entered the "round room" the door behind them shut with a "bang." Everyone jumped, cried out, and fled the house. As the others ran to the truck, however, Jerry stopped and looked back. He could clearly see the outline of a man standing in the room where they'd just been, watching them run. The man had a white glow around him, a soft light that lit up the window. As Jerry watched in horror, the man disappeared.

MY STORY

I, myself, have had a few interesting experiences at Westover. Although I never saw anything, I was once inside alone when I heard something I'll never forget.

I was downstairs in the "round room" when I heard someone walking around above me. There is a large room off the pyramidal room on the second floor, and I'd never felt comfortable in that particular room. On that particular day, I could clearly hear the person walk into that room and then pause, as though stopping for something or someone, before continuing.

I listened as they continued pacing back and forth, as though they were simply carrying on with a mission. It was the oddest thing to hear something so clearly when I knew there was nothing there that should be capable of making such a sound.

I was a teenager at the time and taking photos. Suddenly feeling unsafe, I turned and started for the front door. I'd almost reached the porch when the whole house filled with the sound of singing. It was a woman's voice, rather low and sweet.

I didn't know the song, but it sounded like an old tune; the melody certainly wasn't a contemporary one. It was such a sad noise and the woman singing it sounded as though her heart was breaking. The voice was hollow and seemed to be coming from every direction at once.

I didn't stay around long to listen.

On other occasions, I would touch the wall as I traveled down the narrow, back staircase or put my hand on the curling wallpaper in one of the upstairs rooms and get hit by a terrible sense of sadness.

It sounded silly at the time, but I always felt like the house was unhappy, distraught over its abandoned condition that was getting worse by the day.

SUZIE'S STORY

The following story was sent to me by Suzie Ratliff, a friend and fellow writer who contributed several tales for the book.

"I had parked my crappy Cavalier around the block and snuck in through the tall grass that covered the unkempt backyard of this beautiful structure, just as I had done so on many ventures there. I knew my path to the front porch quite well, even in the dark of the starless night that accompanied me on this eventful journey.

"This home had graced me with her forgotten beauty many times before since my teenage rebellion had led me to the habit of hanging out in forbidden places. As I always did, I stepped carefully up the crumbling stairs to the porch and slowly pushed the ancient French doors that opened to the parlor, shutting them firmly behind me as I headed up the loudly creaking stairs.

"Backpack loaded with my sketchbook, some art supplies, a pack of Lucky Strikes and my trusty zippo, I made the same trip to the turret room as I had made so many times before.

"That was my name for it, the "turret room," as I had claimed it as mine in my silly teenage mind. It was a place where I went to escape, a place where I could sit and just make sense of the world around me.

"People talked about how that place was so haunted, and they'd made it a place where ignorant local teens would go to act foolishly and vandalize this lovely home; I saw a bit of that myself and always ran the idiots off when I could. I loved this place and felt safe within her crumbling confines; she was a grand old gal that had been forgotten and left to fall into ruin.

"The creaking of the stairs woke me from my sleep; the blue light filled the room for a moment and then drew back down the narrow steps to the hallway that led me to a part of the house I had never really explored.

"The floors creaked as the light traveled, not like footsteps but more like a low rumble as it moved on through the dusty corridor with me in foolish pursuit. I was no longer chasing the light but trying to follow this entity through the rumbling sound.

"I remember reaching a small servants' door that led me to small, steep staircase that opened in the kitchen. The yellowed paper of the tiny passage was covered in handwritten recipes that I wish I had now– the scrawling of those long-dead servants who kept the family of the home fed.

"Just beyond the door at the bottom of the staircase I thought I heard a noise, a scrape of some kind across the worn wooden hallway of the first floor.

"Driven by teenage bravery, also known as blatant stupidity, I pressed on to find the source of this noise and perhaps find that amazing blue orb once more.

"I found nothing, just the broken plates that had graced the hallway ever since my first trip to the house, pulled from the built-in hutch and broken carelessly by the people that had explored this beautiful structure before and left behind proof of their disrespect.

I walked on cautiously to the front room, frightened and assuming I was about to have some terrifying otherworldly experience...but there was nothing.

"I started to ascend the aging staircase back towards my refuge in the turret room, but something stopped me, like this impenetrable wall of fear and sadness that had suddenly formed over my feet had happily stepped upon many times before.

I hurriedly left with a chill running through my body that was only tempered by the rush of adrenaline as I made my way through the now dewy wet grass, never happier to see that old car and head home.

"I never made it back to that lovely old mansion again as life got in the way, but I always wanted to return.

"I've been to a lot of very interesting places, and I've seen many things that are difficult to explain, but that one will always stick with me.

(By the way, if anyone wants a twenty-year-old sketchbook full of my forgotten "masterpieces" and a pack of Lucky's, they may still be in the turret room where I left them that night...)

So is there only one ghost haunting the house or is it a combination of people who have passed by or through it over the years?

While researching the history of their house, the Nichols' family did manage to uncover a few tidbits of history that might explain some of the hauntings. For instance, they learned that the Smiths had a young female family member named Elsie, a five-year-old child who passed away.

The Nichols refer to the ghost by her name, and she's made several appearances over the years. Graham, according to the *Richmond Register*, has had a few different experiences with Elsie. In one of her most memorable appearances, she got physical with some of the construction workers. Graham and friends were working on an area of the house that hadn't seen renovations since the late nineteenth century when "Elsie" decided to make herself known. She sent one of the young men "flying six or seven feet across the area yelling 'Somebody kicked my butt and pushed me!'"

WHITE HALL

WHITE HALL IS one of Kentucky's most impressive historical sights. Not only is it a gorgeous example of Georgian and Italianate architecture, but it's also the former home of famed (and infamous) emancipationist Cassius Marcellus Clay, aka the "Lion of White Hall". (Not to be confused with the famous boxer of the same name.)

Although Cassius' father Green Clay deserves his own accolades and Cassius' daughter Laura (the first woman to run for Vice President) also has deserved (or unfair considering the lack of attention she receives) praises for her accomplishments, it is Cassius who receives the most notoriety.

Clay's illustrious history is as varied as the stories that surround him.

To begin with, he was minister to Russia during a time of opulence, balls, and splendor. He was also highly responsible for helping the United States secure Alaska as a state, friends with both Abraham Lincoln and the legendary and tragic Romanov family, and, of course, an emancipationist. He also had two daughters, Mary Barr and Laura, who became prominent figures in the women's rights movement.

And then there was his house. Oh, his house.

If you know nothing of Clay's history, then you should, at least, take a stroll around the grounds and marvel at the wonderful architecture (and forty-four rooms) and sheer beauty of the farmland around it.

It was, and remains, a house fit for a king.

On top of Clay's political achievements, he also had quite a colorful personal history. In fact, sometimes his personal history gets overshadowed by his vast political achievements.

Clay often carried pistols and knives for protection, especially since he received death threats throughout his life and more than one person tried to kill him. Later in his life, when he stopped paying his taxes and the authorities came to demand retribution, he went up to his balcony on the front of his mansion and fired a cannon (which he filled with nails, bits of broken glass, etc.) at them.

His paranoia and eccentricity grew as he aged and he became known as a bit of a recluse and enigma.

After forty-five years of marriage, Cassius and his wife Mary Jane Warfield divorced.

Rumor was that a Russian ballerina showed up at their house during a party and bestowed Cassius' illegitimate son upon him. While this story has never officially been verified, he did adopt a Russian "orphan" by the name of "Launey" (who lived his adult life in a modest house on Main Street in Richmond, although his mother never seemed to materialize again).

And then there is the lovely, intriguing portrait of the half-nude ballerina hanging in his study that has led to much thought-provoking... speculation.

Nearly twenty years after his divorce from Mary Jane, an 84-year-old Clay married 15-year-old Dora Richardson. Naturally, there has been much speculation about that arrangement as well.

Still quite spry in his old age, he once killed two burglars who broke into his study while he napped. Not only was Clay elderly at the time–he suffered from gout as well.

White Hall is a towering, imposing mansion on the outskirts of Richmond. Part of the home, known as "Clermont" was built in the late 1790s by Cassius' father, Green. It became "White Hall" in the 1860s after many additions were included making it much more opulent. Visitors are almost always taken aback and impressed by its stunning architecture, tasteful furnishings (much original to the home), and glorious bucolic setting.

Of course, there's also the ghosts. White Hall is considered to be one of the most haunted places in the entire state.

So who haunts the old mansion? And what happens during the incidents?

There are many possibilities. Several of Cassius' children died in the house, including a 16-year-old son from typhoid fever. Clay's father, Green Clay, died there as well. Then, of course, there were the slaves and tenant farmers who almost certainly passed away on the property.

So the possibilities are endless.

Visitors and staff alike have experienced paranormal activity inside the luxurious walls. Orbs have been spotted flying around the rooms, and some have been captured on film. Lights have been known to inexplicably turn off and on by themselves. Frequently, guests are treated to the baffling aroma of pipe smoke, cigar smoke, the scent of brandy, and more ladylike perfumes that linger in the air.

Before the state restored the mansion to its former splendor and opened it as the museum it is today, the house was empty for many years. It fell into great disrepair. In fact, chickens were found roosting inside the grand piano, which had remained in the "ballroom."

Before it befell to that state of disrepair, the house and land around it was rented out to sharecroppers or "tenant farmers." Some of the ghost stories date back to this period.

"Georgia" offered me the following story regarding her grandmother, who was a tenant farmer at the house...

"My grandmother used to tell me stories about how she'd hear a baby crying at night. Sometimes she'd hear someone pacing back and forth, trying to comfort the child. The footsteps and crying would continue all night long."

LINDSEY'S STORY

"Lindsey", a former tour guide, offered me the following tale about her time working in the house...

"It was a rainy and gloomy day, and we hadn't had a lot of people come through on the tours. It was getting towards the end of the day, and I said I'd lock up. Everyone else left, and I was alone in the house. We didn't get another tour, so I went up to the third floor to my dressing room and started getting out of my costume.

"A few minutes later I heard footsteps coming up the stairs. They stopped on the second floor. I thought it might have been the maintenance worker or maybe another guide coming back inside. But then they called my name.

"It was a man's voice, but I didn't recognize it. I stopped and walked over to the landing and looked down. I could see the shadow of a tall man down there but couldn't see a face. I called back and answered by the guy didn't move. Started getting a little freaked then, so I finished getting dressed. As I walked back towards the stairs, the voice came again. This time, it called my name and asked where I was. I flew down the stairs and looked, but nobody was there; nobody was in the house at all."

MY STORY

As a former tour guide myself, I have my own story to tell about the house...

I was a tour guide at White Hall during the late 1990s and have my own story about its otherworldly inhabitants.

One incredibly hot summer afternoon I was busy trying not to wilt and pass out while still trying to give an interesting, informative tour to three men from Canada. We'd been through most of the house, including the stifling third floor, and were getting to the end and walking down the back staircase.

I was leading the way and about four steps from the bottom when I found myself coming to an abrupt halt. Not ten feet in front of me was a woman in a long white dress standing in the middle of the dining room. I watched as she danced through the doorway into the foyer and then glided across the floor to the ballroom.

I was quite surprised since not only was I the only female working that day, I was, therefore, the only one in costume. But the lady before me, her feet never really seemed to touch the ground. It was very odd, and the sweat that was pouring down my hot face and back turned to ice.

I didn't say anything to the guys behind me. I kind of thought, and probably hoped, that it might just be my imagination or maybe even heat stroke. The day had been unbearably long, and it was almost hot enough to fry eggs on the sidewalk. Of course, this back before the house was fully air-conditioned and those many-layered costumes on top of the stuffy house could get to you by the end of the day.

At any rate, I finished the tour in the basement and then guided the men outside. Before they headed off to the summer kitchen, however, they turned back to me and said, "There's something we want to ask you…"

In hushed voices, they proceeded to tell me that all three of them had seen the woman as well. They'd assumed she was part of the tour.

Another story was offered to me by a woman who was not a tour guide for the mansion, but a guide during the "Ghost Walk" the EKU theater department often puts on each Halloween at the mansion. This is her tale...

I was a Ghost Walk guide for two years in a row. I didn't have anything unusual happen that first year, but in the second year, something really strange occurred. After that, I never tried out for it again.

It was getting late in the night, and I had just finished my final tour. I wrapped up with everyone outside, and my group was drinking their cider and eating their cookies. I suddenly remembered that I'd forgotten to secure a ride home, so I excused myself and went back up to the second floor with the intentions of talking to one of the actors who sometimes offered me a ride. They were in between tours, so I knew if I went right then I wouldn't be interrupting anything.

I got up to the second floor where there was this huge mirror on the landing. The house wasn't dark or anything but the little lamps that were on kind of made all these shadows everywhere. Something in the mirror made me stop and take a second look.

For just a second, I swore I saw a woman standing behind me in the reflection. She was tall and wore a long dark dress. And she was following me.

And then, for a reason I can't explain, I forgot about my ride and began walking up the smaller set of stairs to the nursery. I walked into that room and just stood in the middle of the floor and looked around. The feeling I got was terrible– like my chest was being crushed. I began having a horrible anxiety attack and almost passed out.

And then I saw the woman again out of the corner of my eye.

I swear I felt like I was in a trance the whole time. I left the house and never went back inside again.

So who is haunting White Hall? Or what? And how many of them are there?

At least three different ghosts purportedly haunt the mansion: a woman in a long black dress (and sometimes in a white dress), a child (probably a boy), and Cassius himself.

Cassius is the most identifiable, recognized by the scent of his smoke and brandy which randomly fill the room and by his voice that has called out to more than one staff member by name.

The woman may or may not be Mary Jane Warfield Clay. Nobody is quite sure who she is, but she's been seen on many occasions. It's also possible that she is a former nanny to the Clays. The nursery is one room in the house that has hosted paranormal activity. I, myself, feel uneasy in that room. There were many times during both a regular tour and a Ghost Walk tour (for which I was also a guide) in which I'd find myself standing in the middle of the room and suddenly feel at a loss of breath. Like Claire said in her story, there is pressure in that room, a darkness, that's never felt good.

I once brought a friend up there with me, a nonbeliever, and after several seconds of standing there he walked out mumbling, "Must be some kind of roof slant or something..."

But I didn't think so then and still don't today.

The grounds have lots of potential ghosts, of course. In addition to the Clay family who could be haunting it, there is also the man Cassius shot and killed, the children who didn't survive infancy, slaves, and tenant farmers who are all likely suspects for ghosts.

In the book *Cassius M. Clay* by local author Keven McQueen, McQueen interviewed "Addie D." whose father was born in the house and whose family were tenant farmers there. According to him, there was a "ghostly woman" who appeared in the house on a regular basis, and he and other occupants regularly saw floating lights as though "someone was carrying a lantern" (McQueen, 74). McQueen also reports that when renovations were going on in the 1960s, guards often spotted a light, like a candle, moving from window to window at night.

In addition to the strange scents, mysterious lights, and floating lights, staff members have also reported hearing the sounds of what can only be described as "parties" going on inside the house when nobody else is there.

WACO TALES

WACO MIGHT BE one of the smaller hamlets within Madison County, but it is not without its own strange and unusual tales. Here, we will attempt to uncover just a few of the stories that take place in and around Waco. But first...

A couple of years ago, when I first began researching material for the book, someone told me that Panola was haunted by "witches" who were burned to death for their "crimes."

Only one person shared this tidbit of information with me and I have been unable to verify it in any way, shape, or form—either through local storytellers or historical sources. I even ended up interviewing people in and around Panola who had been there for generations, but it was to no avail.

THE MOBERLY HANGING MAN

Although it's not quite Waco, one story that continued to pop up in my research was that of the "hanging man." And, like many of these stories, this one ended up having quite a bit of truth to it.

Several people in Moberly and Speedwell told me the story about a hanging man whose body you can still sometimes see in a field. More importantly, at least to the storytellers, you can evidently *smell* him...

JASON'S STORY

"Jason" is a lifelong resident of Speedwell. He shared the following story about the "hanging man" and his own personal experience with the ghost. I have left his tale in his own words, as submitted to me via my Haunted Estill County *Facebook page.*

"I've heard about the hanging man all my life. It happened over there at Moberly. A man and woman were out in the field and saw something in a tree.

"They thought it was a monster, at first, and it smelled terrible. When they got closer to it, though, they saw it was a dead body hanging from the tree. It had been there for months. Some people say you can still see it.

"I never believed it but then, when I was sixteen, I was visiting a cousin who lives over there. We were walking around, smoking, and it was about 10:00 pm. All of a sudden, we got this terrible smell that hit us. It was like raw sewage or something. Just awful. That's when my cousin shouted and pointed.

"I looked up, and there was a tree about twenty feet in front of us. Sure enough, it looked like a dead body swinging from it. The smell was like nothing I'd ever been around before, but later we had a cow die and it was the same smell. The thing in the tree disappeared after about a second. I thought maybe it was just the moon playing tricks, but now I'm not so sure."

Like many of the ghost stories here in the book, there is some truth to the original tale associated with this one. There was, in fact, a man whose body was discovered in Moberly many years ago, in pretty much the same state as Jason and others described to me.

In 1906, Joseph Walker Fry's body was discovered hanging from a tree. The coroner estimated his body had been there for about four months. Fry's body was cut down, examined right there on the ground by the tree, and subsequently buried at Speedwell. Nobody was sure what happened to him or why he was hanging from the tree–whether it was a homicide or suicide, although some relatives admitted to the local paper that he'd been drinking heavily recently.

THE WACO SPY

The Civil War was a terrible time for just about everyone involved. It was not a good time, and horrible fates befell to innocent people, either in the name of war, fear, or paranoia. Although the Battle of Richmond is considered the county's most important part of the war, it's not the only story to come out of that time.

Things hit close to home when a poor, innocent Waco man was accused of being a spy and subsequently hanged for his "crime."

E.S. Dodd was a Confederate soldier, a private in Co. D of Terry's Texas Rangers fighting in East Tennessee under Confederate Gen. Longstreet. His parents were Travis and Nannie Dodd, and they lived east of Waco.

During the war, their son sent them several letters chronicling the terrors and dangers he'd seen and faced. However, his last letter was the most horrifying. On Jan. 6, 1864, Private Dodd and several others became separated from their command while they were taking a cavalry supply wagon train to Loudon, Tennessee. When Federal troops took the area, the Confederate wagon train left without Private Dodd and the others.

They traveled for many miles, finding shelter with southern sympathizers. Around Sevierville, Tennessee, however, Home Guards captured them. Private Dodd, who was wearing his Confederate shirt and pants and a blue U.S. Army overcoat that he had found (and just put on to keep warm), was transported to Knoxville. Although there was no evidence supporting the charges, other than the overcoat that didn't even originally belong to him, he was tried as a spy.

To his parents he wrote that "They have sentenced me to be hanged as a spy day after tomorrow between 10 a.m. and 2 p.m."

You can view the original article at:

Dr. Robert Grise, "Hung as a Spy," Madison's Heritage Online, accessed November 19, 2015, http://library-old.eku.edu/blogs/digital/items/show/1480.

SWEET MISS SARAH

The following story was submitted by Suzie Ratliff, formerly of Waco. I have left the story in her own words, editing only for formatting purposes.

"I turned fourteen the year that we moved into that aging farmhouse so far from town that I thought I'd never see another soul again other than being at school. Big exciting Waco, Ky is where every teen wants to be…right?

"We began renovating the house as soon as we moved in, one heck of a messy job for a family who was trying to do it themselves. The people who had owned the house were both deceased; the house left to waste away despite its former glory. We tore into walls insulated with only newspapers, some of them being absolutely amazing. I'll always wonder what happened to that old yellowed newspaper we found with an article on the front page about the Titanic sinking, yeah, let that sink in. Pun intended.

"I don't have the words to accurately describe what I saw the night that Miss Sarah first visited me, appearing at the end of my bed and nearly scaring the life from my young body. I awoke to see this strange cloudy figure to the right of my bed moving towards me, but instead of being afraid I suddenly felt more okay than I had in a long time.

"This ghost, this reminder of who she once was, stood next to my bed for the longest time. There was no glowing light, no orb; this spirit was far more substantial than that, through a dark grey haze I could make out her figure and matronly face. She made me feel safe, even though the rational part of my mind told me to be afraid of this odd occurrence. I fell back asleep that night with this apparition next to my bed, and it sure wasn't the last time that I would fall asleep that way.

"I ended up giving this kind spirit the name Miss Sarah after the woman who had owned the house before. Of course, I don't know if that's who she once was, but I think that name worked for both of us.

"No one believed me about Miss Sarah. Instead, it became a running joke in our home anytime that something was misplaced, which was constant. But I had unwavering faith in her existence, her choice to remain in this house that had been her home for far more years than I had seen life on this planet.

"When I went to upstairs to my room each night, I was comforted knowing that she would be there to watch over my fitful sleep. That ghost was the guardian of my soul when the nights got too long, even if I was the only one that truly believed in her. I stand by the thought that she was certainly not the only spirit in that dwelling; she was a powerful entity that emanated peace to those she visited and bravely warded away the bad spirits.

"Fast forward two years later when I sent my first car flipping through the ditch down the road not even a mile from the house due to being young and dumb. Hanging upside down from my seatbelt in the ditch drifting in and out of consciousness, I heard Miss Sarah's voice for the first time, "Wake up, you have to wake up."

"In all of my experiences with this entity I had never heard her voice, just her presence and an implied notion of her thoughts. This time, it was just her voice, and its urgency brought me back enough to crawl out of the wreckage and then her voice was gone as soon as I managed to free myself from the crumpled remains of my car.

"I left home shortly after this, but though I left Miss Sarah behind she wasn't done tending to those that lived in her house.

"I lost contact with my family after moving, so this part of the story is simply word of mouth. My stepfather died of cancer in that house a few years after I left; his last months were accompanied by many visits from spirits, as often happens with the dying. From the accounts I heard from my estranged family, his last few days were plagued by demons that made him scream out with fear even under heavy sedation. But sometimes he would get calm and quiet, muttering softly about the nice lady that had come to take him home.

"I like to believe that my sweet ghost Sarah guided him through death to a happier place, to a better plane of existence.

"Thank you, Miss Sarah, for your exceptional service in the afterlife; we need more spirits like you."

THE ELLISTON FARM HOUSE

The last Waco story is from me. For a couple of years, we lived in a large greenish farm house located by the little waterfall as you cross over the bridge into Waco. It's near Waco Baptist Church and is a beautiful house, although we had more than our fair share of supernatural experiences there.

Although we often caught movements from the corners of our eyes, heard strange noises, and had objects inexplicably move on their own, it was what happened when my infant daughter was sick that was the strangest.

My youngest son died of SIDS when he was seven weeks old so, of course, we were extra cautious when our daughter was born a year later.

At four months old she caught a little cold, and we'd been watching her like a hawk. She was restless, not sleeping well, and miserable, but I'd finally gotten her to sleep. I placed her in her crib upstairs, but I was too wound up to sleep myself.

Worried about her, I decided to sit up downstairs and watch television. It was around 2:00 am and I was up alone, my mother (who stayed with us) was asleep in her room, and my husband and son were upstairs. I had both lamps on in the living room and the television on "low" in case my daughter cried.

Suddenly, the overhead light came on. The glare had me jumping about three feet in the air. Not only was I surprised that it had come on, we had never been able to find that switch, so it had never been on.

I waited for a few seconds and then heard my daughter whimper upstairs. I ran up, soothed her, and put her back to sleep.

The light went out on its own.

An hour later, as I was dozing, the light snapped on again.

I woke up with a start and immediately thought of my daughter. When I got upstairs, I found her unresponsive, not breathing.

My mother and I rushed her to the hospital where the doctors administered oxygen and antibiotics.

The light never came on again.

THE CANE PATCH MURDER

CLOSE TO THE Blue Grass Army Depot, there was a farm several decades ago that no longer exists. A man and woman lived there, but they were apparently unhappy.

One night, for reasons nobody ever understood, the man killed his wife by chopping off her head. He buried her body on the farm but didn't bury her head with the body. Now, supposedly, you can find her walking along US 52 and on the backroads behind the Depot, looking for her head.

So, truth or fiction?

Unfortunately, at least, part of this tale is true.

There truly was a murder in this area that resulted in the husband killing his wife in such a morbid manner. The story has grown into a legend over time, however, and few people probably realize that something did happen (although not exactly in the way the story is told).

At dusk on Friday, September 18, 1936, a tenant laborer named Stanley Isaacs (or Harry Brotherton, depending upon the source) was walking home after a long day's work at cutting corn in Madison County, Kentucky. Possibly Isaacs was whistling a tune, as men tend to do after working hard, and imagining that all was right with the world. As he sauntered by a sugar cane patch located on Percy Maupin's farm near Stagner Lane, six miles from Richmond, Isaacs received his first hint that something was awry.

Something didn't sit well with him when he glanced at a pair of black women's shoes for the third time. He'd seen them lying in the ditch since Wednesday. Today, however, a horrible stench permeated the air near the shoes and made him gag and a pair of dogs ran out of the nearby cane patch and tried to attack him.

Isaacs decided to investigate further.

What he found left him shocked. There, with hardly any flesh covering the bones on her face, was a woman's head. Her hair was gone, and there was nothing distinguishable about her.

Authorities were called in.

When the rest of the body was discovered, they found that the body's left arm and right hand were chopped away (Cincinnati Enquirer, 1936). It took quite some time to locate them.

Parkie Denney was accused of murdering his wife and cutting her body up into pieces. He was eventually executed for his crime.

In a rather bizarre end to the tale, before they figured out who she was, her head was left in a bucket of fluid on the back porch of the funeral home for several weeks.

With that being said, there are some who swear that they've seen the poor woman's ghost wandering down the road at midnight on Halloween.

DANA'S STORY

"Dana" told me about her husband's experience with the headless woman not long after I began the research for this book...

"Dana" told me that her husband, a local police officer, was driving home one night when he saw a woman up ahead of him in his headlights. She was walking very slowly, like she was injured, and wearing a long black coat. From a distance, she appeared "normal" looking, although she was swaying from side to side a little and he thought she might be inebriated.

As his cruiser closed in on her, he saw something he will never forget: from the shoulders down the woman looked completely normal from the back.

But she was missing her head.

He went up the road about twenty feet and turned around, hoping to see her from the front. He thought, and hoped it was a trick of light or she was wearing a costume. When he started back down the road towards where she'd been, however, she was gone.

DOLORES' STORY

Dolores Eades told me the following story about the ghost of the headless woman.

Dana wasn't the only person who shared the tale of the headless woman with me. Only, in this case, the woman wasn't necessarily missing her head–she was missing her face!

At the time of the story, Delores' husband was working for the electric company. It was way down in the fall, and one of his co-workers jokingly told him, "Now don't go out on Crooksville on Halloween night, or you won't like what you see!"

Naturally, this piqued Dolores' husband's curiosity. What might he see on Halloween night on the other side of the Depot?

Well, apparently, as the story was told to him, a woman got into a fight with her husband, and he chopped her to pieces, her body parts scattered all over the corn field and buried under the stalks.

The man telling the tale had had his own experience with the headless woman himself.

One night, while driving down Crooksville Road, he saw a woman in a long black cloak walking along the side of the road.

When she he slowed down to ask her if she needed any help, she turned and looked at him...and had no face!

When Delores spoke to her parents that night about the tale her husband had just been told, one looked at the other and said, "I wonder if that was poor Ms. Alcorn?"

So, is there a headless woman walking up and down Crooksville on Halloween? And, if so, what's the rest of the story?

The interesting thing about this story is that it's an older one and not a tale that the younger generation seems to be familiar with, unlike some of the other urban legends. I know that I, for one, had not heard of it until I began researching stories for the book, and Dolores Eades gave me her tale. However, as I began interviewing county residents who have lived in or around Madison County since the 1940s or earlier, the headless woman tale appeared to be pretty prevalent. So, somewhere along the way, it got lost. Ironically, there is some truth to this story, which makes it, even more, gruesome...

The actual details of the story are about as gruesome as the can come, and are not something one would think of hearing about in the Depression-era Madison County.

In 1936, a nearly nude headless body was discovered off of Stagner Lane. Although I have not been able to locate a "Stagner Lane" on any recent map of the county, I am fairly certain it was around Crooksville Road or the Muddy Creek area or is more likely enclosed within the Depot's compound. Considering that it was "12 miles east of Richmond" that would almost put it near the Estill County line although the crime that took place was definitely on the Madison County side.

Now, for those history buffs, I did locate some information that would suggest Stagner Lane was once part of the Bluegrass Army Depot:

"The current project area was previously examined for cultural resources by the Corps and AMEC Earth and Environmental, Inc.... One historic property eligible for listing to the National Register of Historic Places (NRHP) was identified at this time, a historic road known as Stagner Lane. It is described as an embedded, wagon wheel roadway developed by local farmers in the mid 1800's. Though not associated with either Boone's Trace to Boonesborough or the "Wilderness Trail", Stagner Lane was an important element of the cultural landscape for Madison County, Kentucky and the BGAD...This work was completed in 2007 and included the current project area. In addition, two archaeological sites [...] were recorded.... Site 15MA379 is described as the remnants of a historic residence dating to the late nineteenth century. Site 15MA384 is an unknown prehistoric artifact scatter. Neither site was considered eligible for listing to the National Register of Historic Places. Therefore, no further work was recommended. No other cultural resources or historic properties are recorded within the current project area." And then, later, "This *evaluation literature review was conducted IAW the Memorandum of Agreement between United States Army Corps of Engineers, Louisville District, Blue Grass Army Depot and Kentucky State Historic Preservation Office, regarding the remains of Stagner Lane, an abandoned historic roadway within the project area."* (http://www.peoacwa.army.mil/wp-content/uploads/Bluegrass_Supplemental_EA_2011.pdf)

At any rate, before Stagner Lane became part of the Depot, it was witness to its own notoriety.

On September 18, as previously mentioned, a severed head was discovered in 1936 about 400 yards away. For weeks, police didn't have any clues as to what may have happened or even who the victim was and the story, which gained national attention, became known as the "Cane Patch Murder Case."

Eventually, a tip came in and the woman's husband, Parkie Denney, was arrested yet continued to maintain his innocence. He went through four different trials (including one in Clark County and one in Fayette) before a jury could agree on his guilt and subsequent punishment.

Eventually, he was sentenced to death and successively electrocuted at Eddyville on September 2, 1938.

It was Madison County's last execution.

THE GLYNDON HOTEL

AT ONE TIME the Glyndon Hotel, located on Main Street in Richmond, was a real showpiece. It's still a beautiful building, with a stately lobby, quirky rooms, and old-world charms. Unfortunately, it is not currently in use.

Sometimes the guests apparently don't ever check out from the rooms. Many people who have worked at the former hotel or stayed there as guests have tales to share about the invisible inhabitants.

Some former employees and guests have mentioned strange noises at night that sounded as though people were in the rooms, going about their business, even though the rooms were empty. Former desk workers talk of staying up late at night (my own husband was a night desk worker until the hotel closed) and hearing footsteps going up and down the stairs, even when the hotel didn't have a single guest.

I would like to spend a bit of time talking about the old hotel but, unfortunately, not everyone likes having ghost stories shared about their establishment. My husband is a former employee of the hotel, as well as another business operated by the owner. When our youngest son died unexpectedly, our family was treated very, very well by the hotel's owners. For that reason, I will respect privacy wishes.

However, since this IS a book about haunted places, I'll share a quick tidbit I came across during research: supposedly, the when the Lindbergh baby's killer was being executed, people gathered at the hotel to listen to the radio broadcast and, during the broadcast, the clock hands in one of the rooms stopped and never moved again...

A FUN NIGHT AT THE OPERA

AND NOW, for a quick break from the ghosts–something a little different and quirky from Richmond's past...

It is hard to believe that there was once an opera house on Main Street and Richmond and that it hosted Hollywood "stars" right there in Richmond. Well, sort of...

In 1937, The Richmond Daily Register reported that "All the fanfare, the brilliance and the realness of a veritable Hollywood Premiere will be reproduced in all its regal splendor Tuesday night at the Madison Theatre here in Richmond. The Hollywood Premiere will be presented in true Hollywood style with special floodlights illuminating both the front of the theatre and the stars."

Of course, they weren't the "real" stars from the silver screen–they were impersonators from EKU. Still, stars such as Clark Gable, Shirley Temple, Mae West, and Ginger Rogers were represented and made their way down the red carpet amidst paparazzi and autograph hounds.

Apparently, even though they weren't the real people, the citizens of Richmond didn't care at all and still made a fuss. In the September 29, 1937, issue of the Daily Register, it was reported that "Policemen had difficulty keeping the crowds away from the entrance of Madison Theater last night as the Schine's Theater management presented a 'Hollywood Premiere.' The spectacle, a Rob Gage presentation staged by Josephine James drew autograph seekers, celebrity hunters and others who came to get a glimpse of their favorite movie star. Inside the theater was a crowd equal to the one outside."

It was a much simpler time then.

There were many similar events held in downtown Richmond "back in the day." After the Civil War, for instance, a "peace ball" was held downtown to promote amity and civility between the two sides.

(You can read the entire article about the celebrities at: Dr. Fred Engle, "Hollywood in Richmond," Madison's Heritage Online, accessed November 19, 2015, http://library-old.eku.edu/blogs/digital/items/show/1464)

LITTLE EGYPT

EVERY COUNTY HAS their own handful of urban legends, and, at least, one of them is usually a variation of the following tale. This is the story of Little Egypt and how teenagers for generations now have tried to capture her elusive spirit.

On a clear dark, night, preferably when a full moon is out, adventurous souls can try to meet the spirit of Little Egypt, a local ghost who apparently just wants a ride home...

On Four Mile Road, there is a crossing close to the site of an old farm. Although Four Mile is now full of new developments and subdivisions, when I was a kid it was almost all farmland, once you got past Cottonwood. According to the story, if you stop at just the right spot in the road, roll down your windows, and call for "Little Egypt" an invisible specter is meant to climb into your car, ride on down the road a bit, and then get out just as quickly as she got in.

Lots of souls have tried this over the years, and some even have chilling tales to tell...

THE HAUNTINGS

Like any good urban legend, there are different variations of the haunting and how to make the little ghost girl appear.

In one story, travelers are meant to go to the bridge at midnight, on a rainy night of course. If you call her name three times and tap the two front windows, she will enter the car, feeling like a short burst of wind. You must also crack the two front windows once she's inside. If you don't crack the windows, then she won't be able to escape.

Others say that you must pull onto the bridge on Four Mile Road, stop your vehicle and say "Little Egypt, Little Egypt come ride with me." You will then feel a "presence" enter your vehicle. So what are you meant to do once she enters your car? You're apparently meant to drive her down the road a bit and then turn around and return her to the spot in which you collected her. Some have said they feel her get in and some have not.

LOIS, JULIA, AND LITTLE EGYPT

The following story was sent to me by readers of my Mountain Witch Facebook page.

Lois and Julia (not their real names) decided to try and "meet" Little Egypt back in 1996. It was around 10:00 pm on a Friday night and they were college freshmen at the time. They'd already driven out there earlier in the day, to see the bridge where they were meant to stop, so they knew where they were meant to be going.

Of course, things looked different in the daylight.

Once they reached the bridge both said they could feel cold chills running up and down their arms. "We hadn't done anything yet, but I guess we'd just spooked ourselves," Julia said. "We almost chickened out but then thought, you know; it was all probably just a joke anyway."

Both girls said the name rice and then asked Little Egypt to get in their car with them.

"At first, we didn't see or hear anything. We couldn't stop laughing," Lois said. "But then the radio, which we had off, came on. It started flipping through the channels. And we really did feel like someone was in the car with us."

They drove up the road a little bit, turned around, and then quickly headed back to Richmond.

"We just hoped that we didn't bring something back to the dorm with us that we shouldn't have," Julia said.

CHRIS' STORY

Chris Meadows sent me the following story about his experience with Little Egypt. I have left it in his own words...

"First and foremost, I am an amateur paranormal investigator. I moved to my parents' house in Berea and I started working at the candle factory where I met my buddy. We'd hang out almost every weekend.

"Well, the weird thing about investigating is once you've caught the bug you've *really* got it, so I started researching different [creepy] places in Madison County and came across the Little Egypt story.

"So [one night] we went to the cemetery on Four Mile and rolled the windows down then drove off and rolled the windows back up. We didn't get but barely out of eyeshot from the cemetery when we both felt like our heads were being squashed by hands or something; I mean, *really* squashed–tears were coming out.

"Finally, I rolled my window down and [the sensation] just disappeared. We both looked in the mirror after we high-tailed it out of there and our eyes were both bloodshot from our experience. There was no alcohol or drugs involved; I run a tight ship when it comes to investigating.

"So I don't know if Little Egypt got to us or something else did because aside from the [regular stories about the] location I've never read or heard anything like that. (I've heard she'll kill you or cause you to wreck, though, so maybe that was her trying to cause a wreck).

"Still, something didn't feel right because the hands or whatever it was that was putting pressure on my head felt *huge*."

DYLAN'S STORY

Another local man, Dylan, sent the following story to me via my Haunted Estill County *Facebook page...*

"So a small group of my friends lived near the Four Mile Bridge. One night, in the summer of 2012 I was over at one of their houses.

"Having lived there for so long, everyone knew the story of Little Egypt but it was one of those things that we never really took seriously. We had stopped on the bridge pretty often to 'invite' her into the car but, inevitably, someone always opened their window just to be safe.

"On that particular night, we decided to make a run to the store and on our way back we stopped on the bridge. It was just starting to get dark.

"This time, when we invited her in, no one opened their window. On the ride back to the house we casually joked around with one another but there was an overarching uncomfortable feeling in the car.

"We'd been driving for a few minutes when suddenly, out of nowhere, a very large black pickup truck started coming at us in our lane.

"Naturally, to avoid a head-on collision, our driver swerved off the road. We ended up in a ditch and slowly gathered ourselves and got out of the car, kind of puzzled and scared.

"It was something we always wrote off as coincidence but I personally always felt the only explanation was that it was her way of trying to get out of our vehicle."

One group of paranormal investigators believe they picked up confirmation of her haunting via EVP. At the following link, you can listen to the evidence yourself:

https://www.youtube.com/watch?v=nzKB9TPSwnc

WHO WAS LITTLE EGYPT?

So who was Little Egypt? Is she simply a figment of our collective imaginations? A ghost girl made up many years ago by an imaginative soul?

Well, some of the story associated with her haunting might be true. And, of course, there are various variations of the tale, so it's hard to separate fact from fiction now.

In one version, the girl's nickname was "Little Egypt." (We don't know why.) She lived on the farm by the bridge. When she was sixteen years old, she was raped and subsequently murdered. Now, her spirit haunts the stretch of road where she was captured and attacked. The poor girl is apparently getting into the various cars in an attempt to find the people who killed her. If she doesn't recognize the people in the vehicles as the killers, she will leave.

On Topix.com, on user offers a similar story to the one mentioned above. She says that her great-grandmother told her that the girl who disappeared from the farm was twelve years old. Her body was discovered in a creek bed a few months later; she'd been raped and killed.

The girl's parents, "devastated by the loss", buried their daughter on their land and then hired someone to build stone pillars and carve the words "Little Egypt" on them. When the man they had hired to create the pillars finished making them, however, they discovered him at the foot of one of the posts, dead. In his pocket was a note that read, "Little Egypt Little Egypt I am sorry for what I did, please let me in."

Evidently, he was unable to get through the two pillars because he was one of the men who had raped and killed her. In addition, he had mixed in a keepsake of hers in the stone pillar as he built it since he was afraid someone would discover it and charge him with the murder.

Another story has it that during the 1920s, there were several different families who lived on the farm. They were all related, but distantly so. One of the daughters got pregnant by one of her cousins. It caused a huge scandal. Upon telling her parents whose child it was, they yelled at her and threatened to kill the baby's father. Distraught, she ran from the house and out to the road.

Back then, there was a big curve in the road (eventually straightened when they built the "new" bypass in the late 1990s). She was struck by a driver and killed. For those who stop and pick her up, if you don't return her to the farm then she'll make you wreck on that stretch of road.

And yet, there is also a third variation of the story…

Coming from Four Mile, there is a house on Hunter Lane on the right side of the road. She was abducted from the house, attacked and raped, and hacked into pieces. Her body parts were transported to the area with the curve on Four Mile Road (to the place where there used to be stone pillars indicating a large farm).

There, they remains were scattered in the field. Travelers are meant to stop at the former farm, call her name, and ask her to get in. Travelers are then mean to stop at the bridge and tell her to get out. If you don't, then you might wreck.

There was once a farm by the bridge, and the driveway contained two big, stone pillars. The name of the farm might have been "Little Egypt" which could at least explain where the name came from, if not the story. I have no idea if the stones actually contained those words; although many people have assured me they did, I've yet to see photographic evidence.

THE PIGG HOUSE

ONE OF THE most haunted locations in Madison County is, unfortunately, long gone, leaving nothing behind but charred ground. The Pigg House burnt to the ground in 2006 before many people were able to enjoy the old log house, or even knew of its existence. (It has gained more notoriety since its demise.) Still, the Pigg House lives on in memory and, for some people, in nightmares...

The Pigg House was an old log house in Berea. For ghost hunters and adventure seekers, it was one of the top haunted destinations in the county. In its last few years, it was owned by Berea College but it ultimately burnt down when lightning struck it several years ago before any major plans were able to be made for it. Although the house was located in a beautiful setting and a piece of Madison County history, it was the ghost stories surrounding it that would send the Pigg House into notoriety.

Lewis and Jeremy remember the Pigg House well. They visited it around fifteen years ago, armed with nothing but flashlights and their nerves. They felt a "dark presence" there almost as soon as it came into view. Neither boy, both of whom were only thirteen-years-old at the time, felt good about being there.

Together, they wandered around the property, touching the logs of the old house, and daring each other to run through the dogtrot. At one point when Jeremy went through it by himself, he could have sworn that someone reached out and lightly touched his arm, as though they might be trying to drag him into one of the rooms or, at least, get his attention.

Others have talked about going there even in the daylight and taking pictures, only to return home and finding them full of orbs and other streaks of light. Some visitors reported feeling something that followed them; it wasn't a benevolent thing since it emitted howling sounds and crunched leaves and twigs as it trailed behind.

One group of teenagers went out to the Pigg House, armed with a Ouija board and flashlights, figuring they'd try to communicate with any spirits they could conjure. At first, the group of boys and girls giggled at the things the board was saying. They all just figured that someone within the group was moving the pointer. However, their laughter stopped when all six of the flashlights they'd set up for light all went out simultaneously.

On my *Haunted Estill County* page, "Mandy" told me about a friend of hers who was visiting the house with a male companion. They were inside, alone together, when she felt something watching them. Upon turning around, she was face-to-face with a black shadowy creature who immediately ran off when it realized it had been noticed.

This is the only picture I am able to share of the house. It belongs to the Berea College special collections' archives and can be found at: http://digital.berea.edu/cdm/ref/collection/p272901coll11/id/573 (source sites in "References" at end of book).

J.D.'S STORY

Another friend on my Haunted Estill County *page, "JD," sent me the following story. I have left the tale in his own words.*

"I had camped out there one night on a boy scout trip early 90's or so. Some of us camped out in the yard, some of us camped out inside the cabin itself. I was inside the cabin with the fireplace.

We [had] all heard the supposed story of how the family was murdered and so on, so I was pretty freaked out by that time. When everyone was in bed, I was wide awake, my eyes darting around the room.

The fire had just about died down and then all of a sudden it shot up as if someone put something on it, which they did not. Around that time I started hearing footsteps in the attic. Not creaking like the house was settling, but like someone was walking around up there. It was not heavy enough to be an actual person, but not light enough to be an animal. I literally did not sleep a wink that night."

MORE PIGG STORIES...

That's not the only story involving Boy Scouts and paranormal activity at the house. According to a commenter on the Unusual Kentucky blog, one night at a Boy Scout campout, the campers listened to the sounds of footsteps as they thundered above them (of course, nobody was there). They then watched in horror as flames shot up through the fireplace. On August 22, 2010, another commenter wrote that he would also camp around the house and that it felt "very creepy and extremely cold regardless of how much clothing, or sleeping bags, etc. you were using" (Unusual Kentucky, 2010).

As with any haunted location, there are always torrid stories that get passed around about it; most of them should get taken with a grain of salt. On the Unexplained Mysteries website, one forum poster wrote that he'd heard the Pigg House was built by "a family of settlers or mountaineers or whatever you'd call them." They were, according to this poster, "all massacred one night." So what happened to them? Two theories prevail. The first is that "Indians snuck up on them in the night and killed the man, woman, and daughter."

The second story is much more harrowing. In it, the father lost a lot of money in a poker game. Since he didn't actually have the money he lost, he ran off. The other players, angry, chased after him. Once they reached his house, they raped his daughter and nailed her to the wall, successively killing her. He then killed the man and his wife.

Supposedly, one could still see the nails in the wall where the daughter was hanged (at least until the house burned down).

MADISON MIDDLE SCHOOL

MADISON MIDDLE SCHOOL holds a special place in my heart. It's my old alma mater, and I was the first seventh-grade class in it when it re-opened as a middle school. Lots of good memories there!

The school itself has a long, interesting history. Before it was Madison Middle, it was Madison High School. Long before that, it was a hospital during the Civil War. (This, incidentally, is true–unlike other stories about area buildings that were purported "hospitals" when they were, in fact, not even around in the Civil War.)

There has always been a multitude of ghost stories circulating this old, stately school that overlooks the town from its hillside perch. When I was a student, lots of my friends talked about its "creepy" feeling and how, even with fresh paint and shiny floors, it felt "old and creepy."

Some of my friends even refused to go to the bathroom on the third floor and would, instead, go down to another floor and use that one there. There have reportedly been murders on the third floor of the building, although I've been unable to dig up any specifics about these deaths, or even prove that they are true. Supposedly, one murder involved a teacher in the 1940s. She was apparently killed in room 306 around 1:00 am. A cheerleader was also supposedly murdered (and raped) on the third floor as well, this time in the 1950s.

There is a third story involving a female student who was being bullied by another girl and hit her head on the sink in the bathroom, leading to her death.

When I was a student, some of the girls would talk about how they would be in the bathroom after school, for cheerleading practice or drama club, and hear crying, screaming, and moaning coming from one of the stalls. Others talked about feeling various cold spots in the room.

SHERRY'S STORY

A good friend of mine, "Sherry", was on the drill team and used the "haunted" bathroom to sometimes change clothes in after school was out. I have left her story in her own words.

"It was right after school and I had run to the bathroom to get changed. I didn't like to be in there by myself but there were still some other kids in the hall and stuff so I felt okay.

"When I came out of the stall, though, I got the weirdest feeling that someone was in there with me. I could hear them sniffing and breathing really loudly. Something didn't feel or sound right about it and, I don't know why, but I looked under the stalls. I didn't see any feet. I figured maybe it was the pipes or something or maybe it was the kids out in the hallway.

"Anyway, I was touching up my makeup and realized that everyone out in the hall had gotten real quiet.

"That's when I heard the scream.

"It was so loud that I dropped my mascara wand. I jumped about ten feet up into the air. It scared me to death. It sounded like the person was right in the room with me, just behind one of the stalls.

"Then a burst of cold air just overtook me. It couldn't have been any colder if I'd walked through a freezer.

"I got my stuff together and ran from the bathroom. When I got out into the hallway, the kids were all still out there, making a racket. I don't know why I didn't hear them before. I figured I might have gone back in time or something."

The *Unusual Kentucky* blog has written about Madison Middle School and some of the paranormal activity it's seen over the years. One reader even sent in a picture of an apparition they caught on camera. Supposedly, the picture was taken at 1:00 am when the school should have been empty, yet you can clearly see multiple students in a classroom through one of the windows. Although some commenters argue that it could have been taken during the daytime and Photoshopped and others claim it looks like puppets, for many it's evidence of the paranormal–a class full of attentive students, ready to get their day started.

A RENTAL HORROR

A contributor, Julie Hale Jones, sent in the following stories to use for the book. I've left both stories in her own words. The first story occurred back in the early 1990's at a trailer park off of Keri Ann Court...

"I once lived in a rental trailer in Richmond. There was just a fence and some shrubs that separated the trailer from a grave yard. I knew something was a little "off" almost as soon as we moved in.

"One of the first things I saw were black shadows moving around throughout the day. Then, early one morning after my husband left for work, I was awakened by the sound of both the storm door and front door opening and closing. As I listened, I could hear heavy footsteps walking from the door to my room. They stopped next to my bed. The baby's crib was right inside the bedroom door.

"My first thought was that my husband had come back home. But once the footsteps stopped at my bed, however, I was literally hot with fear. Then, I decided that he hadn't locked the door back and someone had broken in.

"My back was to the bedroom door and the crib. After several minutes I knew I had to do something so I rolled fast to the other side of the bed and suddenly stood, ready to fight.

"But no one was there.

"I searched the entire house but there wasn't anyone there. The door was still locked, but I had a very strange, uneasy feeling that I was not alone.

"So a few days passed and that same feeling didn't go away. I would be doing the dishes and get a creepy feeling, like I was being watched. I'd turn around and see a blur. It was always quick, but it looked like a black shadow person wearing a cloak.

"Finally, I was so afraid I didn't want to be there alone. So my husband had some Christian friends come in to pray and bless the house. After praying several times they would open the door and ask *it* to leave. Each time I would walk through the house and tell them if I still felt it.

"I always did.

"I believe it was hiding at the other end of our trailer, in the master bedroom's bathroom. Once, my husband and I were sitting on the couch and we both literally jumped up screaming because we felt it sit down next to us. You could see the indention on the couch cushion.

"Finally, I felt that it had left. So the friends left, too. I remember it very clearly. Their muffler was broke and their car was *really* loud. After they left I locked the door and sat down. Suddenly, there was a knocking and banging on the glass of the front door. Then it went to the window and continued knocking loudly and banging. We could still hear our friends' car.

"We both went to the door and looked but even though the banging and knocking were going on and we could hear them, there was no one there.

"I refused to stay in the trailer alone from that night on. Shortly after we moved, never to return. The morning after we moved, my husband left to go to work and I went to a friend's house to spend the day. When I opened the door and cautiously stepped outside I had a chill and immediately turned to the shrubs and fence. I felt it staring at me again, as if it were hiding there watching me.

"I *still* have nightmares about it today."

Julie offered another story about a place she lived at near the Paint Lick area, close to the Garrard County line:

"My husband and I moved into an old trailer that was sitting next to a huge old barn on a farm. We had a newborn baby boy. My husband helped the old guy on the farm and, in return, we got free rent. We didn't have much of anything and slept on a mattress we lay on the floor.

"Well, one night it started raining and I awoke hearing a baby cry. It was coming from under the floor. My husband heard it also. Once the rain stopped, the crying stopped.

"I told my dad this but, being a skeptic, he didn't really believe me and said it was probably a cat or something. (Which I knew was not true.) So time went on but every time it rained the same thing happened. Then, one night my parents spent the night with us. We let them sleep on our mattress and it began to rain. It rained all night. The next morning my dad said he believed me 'cause he heard the crying too.

"Not long after that, my brother and dad came to visit. They decided to go for a walk on the farm. I was home alone with the baby. I was hand washing some baby clothes and laying them out on the deck rails to dry in the sun. My dad and brother were heading back to the house. They were coming down the hill and could see the house in front of them.

"Both of them saw what appeared to be a car parked by the front porch and some women dressed in long dresses. The women come on the porch where I was laying clothes out and follow me inside. They looked at each other and said, 'Wonder who the company is?' Then they walked into a small dip where a stream ran and was out of view of the house.

"Once they come back up from the dip, the women and whatever was parked in front of the house was gone. I walked out to the deck as they approached. Dad ask who come.

"Long story short, they got mad at me and thought I was lying when I said no one was there or had come. To this day Dad *still* talks about the visitors I never saw."

THE RICHMOND KANGAROO

AND NOW, FOR another change of pace.

Yes, you read the title correctly.

When I began working on this book, one night at an Elvis impersonator show, my friend Erin looked at me and said, *"Let me tell you about the time I saw a kangaroo on Barnes Mill Road..."*

Naturally, that grabbed my attention, and I *had* to hear more. She told me her tale, and I immediately got to researching it online, trying to find a plausible explanation. While I didn't necessarily find one of *those*, to my surprise I *did* find someone with a similar story.

Kangaroo sightings have apparently been somewhat regular in central Kentucky, going as far back as 1899. Nobody is quite sure why there seem to be Australian mammals in the area, but there isn't always a rational explanation for the majority of things I have uncovered while researching this book.

ERIN'S KANGAROO STORY

The following is Erin's account of her kangaroo sighting (taken directly from her blog). Both Erin and her mother witnessed the kangaroo in Richmond. Both saw the creature around Barnes Mill Road, in the middle of the day, in a busy area.

Monday, April 4, 2011

http://erinsenclave.blogspot.com/2011/04/kangaroos-in-kentucky.html

This morning I called into my favorite radio program, the Z-ROCK 103 Morning Show. The topic being discussed was "Things you tell people that they never believe". On my whole drive into work, I debated calling with my story and then finally broke down and called in with my famous

Kangaroo sightings story. Quite a few people have asked me to go into detail, so here it goes:

When I was a senior in high school (9 years ago...I can't believe it's been that long, sheesh I'm getting old), I was driving home from my boyfriend's house one Saturday night around 1am. I was driving down Barnes Mill Road going back to my mom's house (Richmond folks - this was the in-town Barnes Mill Rd., so I was literally a half mile from campus when this happened) when I noticed something out of the corner of my eye.

I looked over and saw a large animal HOPPING through yards next to my car. All of a sudden it darted from a yard out into the road right in front of my car. I slammed on the brakes and stopped in the middle of the road. The animal stopped as well and I got a perfect look at it for around ten seconds as it stood illuminated in my headlights. It wasn't a dog, it wasn't a deer—it was a freaking *kangaroo*.

We both stared at each other and then it hopped off behind someone's house. I immediately went home and woke my mom up to tell her. She totally didn't believe me and neither did my sister. They both insisted I had seen a dog.

Trust me, if you see a kangaroo, there is no mistaking it for any other animal.

A week goes by and again, it's Saturday night and I'm coming home at 1am from being out with friends.

I see the kangaroo again!

This time, it's hopping around in yards near my mom's house. The next day, I tell other members of my family and friends. No one believes me and joke that I must have been drinking.

A few weeks later, I get a call from my mom one evening. When I answer, she immediately says "I will never doubt you again. I just saw a kangaroo in the backyard".

It turns out, she was taking my dog outside to use the bathroom when Ginger started going nuts, barking near a large bush. My mom said the bush started rustling and shaking and the kangaroo hopped out, looked at her and took off hopping in the opposite direction.

This helped reassure me that I wasn't crazy.

That was the last we've seen of the Richmond, KY Kangaroo.

WHY A KANGAROO?

That is the question we all want to know. The fact is, Kentucky does have legitimate kangaroos. However, they hang out over near Horse Cave at Kentucky Down Under–a zoo of sorts. That isn't anywhere near Richmond. According to Unusual Kentucky, in 1899 wild kangaroos were spotted all over the country, including Northern Kentucky (which still isn't Richmond).

While Erin was on the phone with the radio station, the host did his own research and found that a circus train apparently derailed in Central Kentucky in the late 1800's. In her research, Erin discovered that there were, in fact, three more circus railcars that crashed in Kentucky during that period as well.

Is it possible that a kangaroo family escaped when a circus train derailed and went on to have little kangaroo babies that have been hiding out around Richmond for more than one-hundred years? Or, did someone around Barnes Mill Road have an illegal pet that escaped? Who knows?

Erin isn't the only one who has seen a kangaroo in Richmond, however. An anonymous commenter on her blog wrote:

My husband and I saw something that looked like a Kangaroo in Winchester, the road on our way to Richmond, right about the Madison County line. We were on our way to visit our son at EKU and on that road by Hall's on the River, and we saw something hop across the road. This was in the middle of the day. We weren't the only one because there was a truck in front of us that turned like we did to see if we could "catch it." They did a U-turn on that road like we did. It sure looked like a kangaroo. (Anonymous May 25, 2012, at 9:13 PM)

BLACK HELICOPTERS

THOSE OF US who grew up around the Blue Grass Army Depot know a host of stories about the compound–some real, some not even close to being real. However, one of the more interesting things to come out of Depot Lore is the black helicopter. Many of us have seen at least one; some insist they don't really exist.

So the "black helicopters" made famous on *The X-Files do* exist and they're right here in Richmond. People who live close to the Depot have seen and heard them for years. They can be heard hovering over houses in the middle of the night, seen flying through the sky mid-afternoon, and witnessed at various other intervals throughout the day.

So why are they even considered mysterious if they're so obviously *real*?

According to the *Unusual Kentucky* blog, the helicopters use "special paint." What does this paint do? It apparently offers protection from any chemical attacks but, probably more importantly and more mysteriously to the rest of us, is non-radar reflective. This allows the helicopters to do their thing without showing up on radar. The fact that they are prepared for chemical attacks is a little disturbing to some and, of course, the conspiracy theorists have a range of notions as to what their special "missions" are that would warrant their special paint.

The following is a list of several theories that area residents offered to me as the "missions" of these choppers:

- To check on fault lines, in case of a major earthquake happening and destroying the chemical weapons.
- To spy on area residents.
- To illegally transport chemical weapons.
- To transport international war criminals.
- Looking for "drug farms." (To be fair, this *does* happen in the area, but those helicopters have different markings.)
- To spray chemicals over area residents. (That's about as specific as that theory got.)

The *Unusual Kentucky* blog also gathered several theories regarding happenings at the Depot. Some of theirs included:

1. Alien technology was recovered from a crashed alien spacecraft and is used in "experimental aircraft being tested" there (*Unusual Kentucky*, The Bluegrass Army Depot, 2008).

2. According to one source, not only was there alien spacecraft, but that it was stored underground at the Depot because "They wouldn't keep it where everyone expects it" (*Unusual Kentucky*, The Bluegrass Army Depot, 2008).

3. Many forms of innovative secret aircraft types, including the Stealth Bomber, are apparently tested there onsite. One of the carriers is evidently invisible and works as a monitor *and* a camera.

4. And, lastly, the unnamed source claimed that the Bluegrass Army Depot (yes, the same one in Richmond) is, in fact, the headquarters for Chemical Warfare.

On November 17, 2009 AT 7:42 AM, a commenter called "Ed" on the Unusual Kentucky's blog entry wrote that:

"I've always thought that if such a chemical existed then The Blue Grass Army Depot would be the place where they house the O3 (Tri-Oxen) chemical from The Return of the

Living Dead movies, and the first Return of the Living Dead movie was supposed to be a true story set in Louisville, Kentucky."

Clearly, there is much speculation and little trust as far as what goes on at the Depot, despite the fact that a good number of area residents are employed there and report no suspicious sightings or incidents.

For what it's worth, however, the "invisible" technology on the aircraft carrier actually does exist. The technology is called "Electrochromatic Panels." Sometimes truth really can be stranger than fiction.

RANDOM RICHMOND STORIES

SOMETIMES I COME across stories that don't fit into any one particular category, so that's what this chapter is for: all the random stories about Richmond that just don't seem to go anyplace else.

Supposedly, the Richmond courthouse is haunted by the ghost of a Civil War Colonel. Various courthouse employees have reportedly heard him marching around inside. They have also taken what they thought were normal pictures of the interior and exterior only to have them come back with the outline of a man in period uniform. In addition, the Colonel has been seen walking sadly around the lawn in front of the building. During the Civil War, a fence was placed around the courthouse lawn and "prisoners" were kept behind it. That fence can now be seen in front of the Richmond Cemetery.

A MURDER AND A HANGING

Madison County has seen more than its fair share of grisly murders and miscarriages of justice. It's also seen lots of hangings over the years. Here is one of those tales.

Lewis Eads, a farmer, lived near the mouth of Muddy Creek. He was an old man and carried around a Bowie knife, which he purportedly knew how to use very well. In 1863, he and his wife went to bed as usual. Their grandson Lewis, and a slave named Claibe, slept in the room with them.

Sometime during the night, they were awakened by burglars. A bullet grazed the grandson's head, and several of the burglars began attacking Lewis Sr. Grandson Lewis and Mrs. Eads ran to a neighbor's house for help.

When the men returned to Mr. Eads' house, they found him dead; his body was mutilated. He had also been robbed. Many people ended up pointing a finger at Claibe, the family's slave, and another slave named Perry who lived on a neighboring farm.

A crowd would've lynched the men, but the suspects were taken to jail for justice to be doled out in a different way. When Perry tried to escape, he was removed from the jail and sent to join the Union army.

Claibe had a trial in June 1863. The circumstantial evidence and testimony from the witnesses helped find him guilty. He was sentenced to hang on Aug. 1, 1863.

At the corner of Irvine Street and Four Mile Road, a gallows was constructed. On the day of the hanging, a noose was fixed around his neck as he stood in a wagon. Despite the crowd who'd gathered to watch him pay for the crime, the hanging itself only took a few minutes and was over with quickly. His body was buried at the foot of the gallows.

Claibe never confessed to any crime.

To read more about this case, visit:

Dr. Robert Grise, "A Murder and a Hanging," Madison's Heritage Online, accessed November 1, 2015, http://library-old.eku.edu/blogs/digital/items/show/1406.

In my book *Haunted Estill County* I wrote about several UFO sightings in and around Irvine. Madison County is not immune to the UFO phenomena.

Central Kentucky has been referred to as being a "hotbed for UFO activity." In a 1978 edition of the *National Inquirer* reporter John Cooke even reported that central Kentucky was experiencing a "UFO blitz" and called Madison County part of a "bizarre Bluegrass Triangle." During this so-called "blitz" an office (Trooper Jim Whitaker) over in neighboring Estill County witnessed a UFO while driving through the rural backroads of Irvine. Around the same time. Two Madison County firemen, one of whom being Robert Murphy, were apparently called to put out a grass fire that they claimed to be a "blazing red UFO." The firemen wound up chasing it for over an hour. Murphy described it as a "classic flying-saucer shaped spaceship."

In the same article, seventy-three-year old Elmer Hardy, pastor of Bybee United Methodist Church, encountered a "gigantic, dazzling UFO" on the way to church. Hardy claimed he and his wife were on their way to their Sunday night service when they encountered the UFO.

It appeared to hover above them and was "about 10 stories high and 20 stories wide, with a zillion lights on it."

The UFO appearances continue even today. On the National UFO Reporting Center website one user reports that on 9/18/2014 at 21:58 they saw disc-shaped object above HWY KY25 at 2324 Lexington Road in Richmond. According to their report, the object "slowly traveled in the same elevation to West direction and stopped about 1 mile West from Road KY25 at about 500 feet elevation." It stayed there for around thirteen minutes and then "took off with an unbelievable speed in 45 degree angle" and disappeared.

The object had a dome shape and lights were on the bottom of it - about 8 lights spread in a symmetrical shape. The onlooker reported that the object appeared to "investigate something on the ground" before it quickly left the scene. (NUFORC 9/18/2014).

Another user reported an incident that occurred on 4/19/2014 at 20:47. As the family traveled back to Barbourville through Richmond they witnessed a white light in the sky. They watched as it "went from bright to dull to bright again" (NUFORC 4/19/2014). They were later able to get a closer look at it when they turned a corner and at this time could see a "dark triangular craft with white lights on each of the three corners." Despite its close proximity to the car, the aircraft was quiet and made no noise.

On January 6, 2012, one user even had their own close encounter of the third kind. According to the report (NUFORC 1/8/2012) the witness was smoking in their own backyard in Richmond when they heard a noise by their fence. They initially thought the sound was that of a deer, but as they got closer the witness could tell that they were hearing footsteps that belonged to a person with two feet, not four.

Once they reached the fence, they looked over the top and saw the top of a head that was "fairly large" and pale and seemed to belong to a "3 foot tall figure." When the witness called out to the figure, it "ran away into the woods at a very fast rate and disappeared."

Other locations that have seen UFO sightings in Madison County include: between Lancaster road and Barnes Mill Road west of Interstate-75 above Wilgreen Lake; in the sky above Lake Reba; near The Bluegrass Army Depot; over Wal-Mart; and between Smith Lane and the end of Blue Lick Road in the rural Bobtown/Kingston area.

Filmmaker Jerry Williams has actually made a half-hour film about a supposed UFO "train crash" that occurred in Richmond near the Depot. That film can be found at:

http://ufodigest.com/video/ufo-crash-kentucky

or

https://www.youtube.com/watch?v=MiMxCpjYOMk&feature=youtu.be

THE LIZARD CREATURE

Cryptozoology is a popular topic these days, especially with so many television shows looking for Bigfoot. While Madison County might lack Bigfoot sightings, it does have its own strange creatures that can't be ignored. The "lizard creature" is one of these.

Marvin's Story

According to an account by a witness on the *Kentucky Bigfoot* website, there *is* a creature roaming around Richmond that resembles a "small dinosaur." On 02/11/09 at around 2:00 am, "Marvin" was driving south of Richmond when he saw something he'll never forget. He writes:

"I believe I was south of Richmond, KY. I saw something next to the concrete barrier that divided the north and southbound interstate lanes. I was on the southbound side. I thought, at first, it might be a rabbit, but this thing either jumped the highway or was so fast I didn't see it running. It crossed about 20ft. in front of my truck, easily getting to the other side and disappeared into the woods. I have never seen an animal like this before. I couldn't believe what I was seeing.

"It looked like it didn't have any fur on it, looking like it was just grey skin. It to me looked like a small reptile or even a small dinosaur. It may have been a couple feet or so long. It looked like it had small dark eyes on the side of its head. I also saw a long tail on this thing. It was very very fast and a normal animal I would have hit it, as I was going 65 in a 70-mile speed zone. It happened so fast I didn't notice if it had ears or not. It truly looked like something out of jurisic [sic] park."(Kentucky Bigfoot, 2009).

He goes on to say that it's possible that it may have "come completely across the interstate."

There is also a strange creature that haunts Speedwell. This creature resembles a bird but is much, much larger. "Mandy" sent me a story on my Haunted Estill County page about a friend of hers who saw the creature perched on a fence post. It then swooped down, stood in front of her car, and then flew away. According to someone else in the area, the creature is, at least, six feet tall. Some think it's an experiment from the Depot that has "gone wrong."

HAUNTED CHOLERA GRAVES

Richmond did not escape the 1849 cholera epidemic. Nearly 80 people died in Richmond in just over two months. In those days, the graveyard on Main Street across from Smith Ballard Street was still used. Sometimes the bodies were simply thrown into holes, and unmarked. There were often two or three or even more placed in a single one.

Some residents who have lived around the area, or still do, claim to hear the cries and wails of the sick and scared.

ELMWOOD

Elmwood is the big, beautiful mansion located on Lancaster Avenue and across from Eastern Kentucky University. It is also known as the "Emma Watts Estate." Although it is now owned by the university, the famous story goes that the university's president once asked Emma Watts how much she wanted for her grand house, to which she asked him how much *he* wanted for EKU in response.

Although I don't have any ghost stories about the house that's been uninhabited for several decades, I DO have a fun urban legend about it.

Emma Watts did not have any heirs. All of my life, however, I have heard that she left the house and expansive grounds to her cats in her will. A caretaker was hired to watch both cats AND house. I also grew up hearing that there was a clause in her will stating that the house should never be sold to EKU.

THE TUNNELS

BOTH RICHMOND AND BEREA have their own sets of tunnel lore that can't be ignored.

Most people who grew up in Madison County know about at least one set of underground tunnels; whether the tunnels were real or not was a different story.

Actually, there are some tunnels that really do exist in Madison County. They are considered dangerous these days, however, and not only is it *not* advisable to seek them out, but it's also illegal. Still, here go you– separating fact from fiction...

To begin with, Richmond does have an extensive set of storm drains (like most towns) that will take you over (or under, depending on how you look at it) most of the city. These might not be the exciting tunnels that you grew up hearing about (the ones that connect the entire city and are frequented by monsters of your nightmares and big enough to drive a small automobile through), but they do exist. Unlike big cities, Richmond never had the big sewer system that you see in movies.

Eastern Kentucky University also has its own set of tunnels. Model Laboratory School, for instance, has a few tunnels that once connected the school to Alumni Coliseum and another nearby building or two. It was not an extensive tunnel system, however, and never connected the building to the entire campus.

There are other sets of tunnels on EKU's campus as well that connect some of the older buildings. With some of the buildings now demolished, it's difficult to say if these tunnels still exist.

According to one adventurer, there was an underground tunnel under Model that actually up through a trap door in one of the offices. Kids were known to sneak down there and play games. It has since been boarded up and is no longer usable. (Its original use is not something anyone can verify, although it might date back to the 1960s since there were apparently some supplies down there that dated back to that decade. Some people believe that they were built for safety purposes—as a place for people to go in case of a nerve gas leak or attack.)

In 1998, a friend of mine took me to Danforth Chapel at Berea College and showed me a "secret" entrance to a tunnel that runs under the college. He lifted up the rug and showed me what appeared to be a trap door. Alas, it was locked so I never got to see if it was, in fact, a real tunnel or just an entrance to a storage room.

So what about Berea's tunnels?

Danforth Chapel is located in the Draper Building. Berea College, which was founded in 1855, is said to have been involved in the Underground Railroad. Some people believe that the tunnels under the college were used to hide runaway slaves, although the "underground" part of the railroad was not usually taken quite so…literally. Danforth Chapel as a building does not date back that far, either.

There appears to be another entrance to a "secret tunnel" in the Phelp Stokes Chapel tunnel. Some of the buildings were built on sites of older buildings, so it's possible that there were tunnels, or old cellars, that got sealed over the years.

If the tunnels exist, there could be another reason for their existence. Some believe they were utilized during the time of the "Day Law"–when blacks and whites were not allowed to be educated in the same schools. And some believe that the tunnels were constructed so that the black students could be educated in secret.

Then again, these stories could very well just be part of the urban legends that follow old buildings, old schools, and old towns.

Some of you might enjoy the fact that, while researching the Berea tunnels, I came across someone who was intent on proving that there is an actual railroad in Berea's underground tunnels, complete with tiny track and steam engine.

When a new sewer system was installed in Richmond in 1920, traces of the old Wilderness Road were discovered. The trail is thought to have been one used from the 1790's.

Found under about three feet of pavement, workers discovered a layer of broken rock that corresponded with what we know of the geography and geology of the trail that brought the settlers into this area.

In the 1840's there was apparently a question as to whether or not the road to Lexington should be paved with rock. Some were in favor of an all-weather highway since it would support the heavy wagons and coaches while others thought the rough rock surface would cause vehicles to shake to pieces and make the horses lame.

Those who wanted a dirt road tried to make their point by bringing in wagon loads full of dirt and spreading it out about a foot deep on top of Main Street. A big rainstorm came shortly thereafter and the mud made the street unnavigable. As a result, those who wanted the road paved in rock got their way.

EKU GHOSTS

EASTERN KENTUCKY UNIVERSITY HAS quite a few ghost stories in its own right. From the Pearl Buchanan Theatre to Burnam Hall and even the bathrooms, there seems to be quite a bit of paranormal activity going on. So what happened on the campus and who's haunting it?

BURNAM HALL

One of the oldest dorms on campus, Burnam Hall, is also the dorm with the most ghost stories circling it. Over the years, many residents have claimed to see the spirit of a young woman as she quietly steals down the hallways at night, always disappearing right before anyone approaches her. She's also been spotted in the basement where she walks from one side of the room to the other, as if looking for something.

Who is she? Nobody knows. There are theories, of course.

Lots of young women have lived in the building over the years. Some say that she ended her own life after a difficult break-up with her boyfriend. Others say she committed suicide upon discovering she was pregnant and the shame of possibly disappointing her parents was just too much to bear. And then some just think she was mentally disturbed and hung herself from a water pipe in the basement and wasn't discovered until days later when a maintenance worker stumbled upon her.

Another interesting story about Burnam Hall is that there is an "abandoned hallway" off the recreation room in the basement. It contains dorm rooms, but the whole hallways was supposedly closed off from the rest of the building almost forty years ago. Those who claim it's there say that if you were to get into this hallway and explore the rooms you'd find that they were practically a time capsule with the furniture, decorations, and even bedding untouched.

KEENE HALL

Deaths on campus are not unheard of so it is not unusual that EKU has ghost stories about students who departed abruptly during their time at the university. Keene Hall, the tallest dorm on campus, has one such story about a student who allegedly committed suicide.

Supposedly, in this dorm that sets apart from the rest of the campus proper, a student fell to their death from the sixteenth floor. While I wasn't able to verify that particular tale, I was able to find people who have seen and heard quite a few things on that particular floor. One former resident told me that they lived on the floor below and that they often woke up in the middle of the night to hear someone walking around upstairs and crying, despite the fact the room directly above them was empty.

According to the "Bit of the Bluegrass" website, Keene's residents have also reported "seeing and hearing doorknobs turning by themselves and doors opening and closing without the benefit of any human hand" (Keila Bender, Bit of the Bluegrass, 2010).

One sad story I *can* verify regarding Keene Hall has to do with a former hall director who lived there in the mid-1990s. My mother was the Area Coordinator of Telford and Walters during the 1990s. Not only was there an accidental death of a female student from the 11th-floor window of Telford during that time, but Keen's former hall director passed away as well. Andrew Nevil was one of our family's best friends at the time; he was a charming, attractive, and highly considerate young man. His residents loved him. Unfortunately, in 1996, he died in the Valu Jet Flight 592 plane crash in the Florida Everglades. Andrew was no longer director, he had left three months earlier, and was in Florida for a hockey game. He wasn't meant to be on that flight at all—he'd decided to take an earlier flight back home to surprise his mother for Mother's Day.

THE RESTROOMS

Then, of course, there are the haunted restrooms on campus.

The Bert Combs Building has the most restroom-inspired ghost stories. As a former student and resident of EKU, I have to agree that there is something a little spooky about the restrooms in that building. As a child, my mother was an education student at the University, and I often accompanied her to class. I would never use the restrooms in the Comb's Building alone; I'd always wait until she finished and we were moving on to the next building.

As an adult, I worked as a teacher's assistant in that building and still got nervous using the restrooms on the third floor. On more than one occasion I'd be in a stall and hear what sounded like someone sighing, crying, or giggling several stalls down from me. There was never anyone there.

Supposedly, both sets of men's restrooms on the third and fourth floors of are also haunted. Some men have felt like someone was standing very close to them, watching them, and have been bothered by an unusually acrid odor that has nothing to do with sewage issues (or whatever normally goes on inside a normal bathroom).

MOORE BUILDING

It's not a dorm, but the Moore Building on campus has a fun story of its own. Home to the science department, its claim to fame is a little...unusual to say the least. The ghost that haunts its hallways is not only female, but she doesn't wear any clothes. This ghost is reportedly good looking and always manages to look surprised (probably not as surprised as the people who see her, however) before she vanishes into thin air.

MOZART, THE DOG

Eastern isn't just haunted by people; it's also haunted by a canine.

"Mozart" was a black Irish Setter/Cocker Spaniel. He is known to wander through the Ravine and take himself on walks. Mozart lived on the campus in the 1950s and 1960s and became known as kind of the unofficial mascot. He apparently belonged to a student but when the student graduated, he left his pet in the care of the Burnam Hall dorm director.

Mozart got to know all the buildings on campus, and it wasn't uncommon for him to sit in on classes, enjoy sporting events, and hang out with students as they studied in the Ravine. Lynn Wolfrom, who once taught music at EKU, said that Mozart would "come to class, and when the class period was up he would get up and walk out" (Haney, Eastern Progress, 2003).

He evidently loved his campus so much that when he died he just never left.

ALUMNI HOUSE

Lastly, the Alumni House on Lancaster Avenue has its own ghost. According to a 2005 article in the Eastern Progress, Eastern retiree Ron Wolfe claimed that in 1995 he had an encounter there in the house while he was working alone one night. He was working on the second floor in his office and had just pulled his curtains to when the phone rang downstairs. Wolfe went to answer it and when he returned, the curtains had magically re-opened (Haynes, Eastern Progress, 2005).

SULLIVAN HALL

SULLIVAN HALL IS another dorm on Eastern's campus that has a few ghost stories floating around about it. Sullivan was built in 1912 and named after Jere A. Sullivan, an attorney who supported the idea of establishing public schools in Kentucky.

Although rumors have that it was used as a hospital during the Civil War, the building was obviously not around during that period.

Room 419 is the dorm room that gets cited with the most paranormal activity. This particular ghost's name is supposed to be "Victoria", and she is said to move objects around, amongst other things. Victoria was meant to be a nursing student in the 1960s and hanged herself from the stress of the nursing program.

EMILY'S STORY

The following story about Sullivan Hall was sent to me by Emily Johnson Wilhoit...

Hello, I wanted to share with you what happened a couple of weeks ago...

I'm a custodian at Sullivan Hall, and our break room is down in the basement.

I was sitting in break room alone, and I thought I caught a pop can move on the table to my right. But, I just thought it was my imagination, and shrugged it off....

Within a couple more minutes, however, it happened again and this time the pop can moved a few inches and made a metal scraping sound against the table. *That* got my attention!

Well at that very moment I got chills; every hair on my arms was standing up. I felt like a surge of energy or something flow through me.

I was not scared, though; *I* was more in amazement and awe!!!

I then sat at the edge of my seat and started talking to whatever was there. I introduced myself. [I told it] I worked there and that I felt its presence and knew it was there. I asked it to please move the pop can again to show me that [it was] real. The pop can moved instantly and scraped against table again...

Well, I felt excited and freaked out at the same time, but never scared.

I have since learned that Sullivan was used as a hospital and the basement was used as a temporary morgue at some point after some war...

Someone said a lady committed suicide on 4th floor. Now, I don't know if any of that is true...

CAROL'S STORY

One EKU alumni, "Carol", offered me the following story about her experience in Burnam Hall. I have left the story in her own words.

"I don't know a lot about Burnam Hall, but I lived in Sullivan for four years as an undergrad, and I always got a weird vibe from it. Not only did I live in it, but I was also a night desk worker for three semesters. I worked the graveyard shift. I liked it because it was quiet and by then all the guys were checked out, but it could get lonely. Let me tell you, sitting there at the desk for six hours alone was boring and scary sometimes. Sitting by myself in the lobby was scary. I heard every single noise, some of which never had any rational explanation (I just thought it was an old building, and those make weird sounds). Walking the floors once a night was always kind of scary, too. Even though you knew that there were girls on the other sides of the doors, you still felt alone.

"The scariest part, however, was going down in the basement. Sometimes I would get this terrifying feeling that someone would lock me in down there, and I wouldn't be able to get out. It didn't help that one of the other desk workers told me about a secret room in the basement that would actually lock you in if you let the door shut behind you.

"Anyway, one night I was working the front desk and I got this feeling that someone was watching me. I hadn't heard anyone come into the lobby, so I was surprised when I looked up and saw this girl sitting in one of the chairs. She had her back to me, but her hair was up on top of her head, kind of old-fashioned looking. She wasn't doing anything, just staring straight ahead. I figured she was waiting for someone. I heard something behind me then and turned around. I swear it was just for a second but when I looked back, the girl was gone."

On The Crypto Crew's paranormal-based website, Andrew Beck, a former student, took a very creepy photo in

Sullivan Hall and posted it online. You can see the photo yourself at:

http://www.thecryptocrew.com/2012/10/ghost-caught-in-photo-at-sullivan-hall.html

It certainly appears as though he has caught a spectre, or some kind of creature, although whether it's a "real" ghost or a simple trick of the light (or even Photoshop) is, of course, open to speculation.

CLAY HALL

THE FOLLOWING STORY was sent to me by Margaret Sowards, a native of Harlan County and a former student at Eastern Kentucky University. This is about her time in Clay Hall...

***

"When I was 18 I moved away from my home of Harlan to attend Eastern Kentucky University in the "big" city of Richmond.

"I feel that my college experience was of the norm in comparison to my peers. I lived in Clay Hall on the first floor with a roommate. We will call her 'Casey'. We got along well and dorm life was fun and exciting. The rooms in Clay Hall had bunk beds and two desks along the right wall when gazing in from the door, and a sink with matching closets along the left wall. A large window covered the far wall.

"Casey was a slender, beautiful girl. I, conversely, was heavier and clumsy, so I was naturally happy when she wanted the top bunk.

"We would often talk into the wee hours of the night, her on the bunk above me. In the darkness, only our voices allowed us to know that the other was there.

"One night, I was awoken by Casey's voice. There was a tremble and meekness to it. 'Margaret, where are you?'

'I'm in bed,' I started to answer but before I could finish she began to cry and call out.

'What's wrong Casey?' I asked as I sat straight up in the bed, hitting my head on the bunk.

'There's someone in the room! There's someone standing in front of the mirror!' Her voice came softly through the blackness of the room.

"I looked around but couldn't see anyone. I slowly got out of bed as I listened to my roommate cry and plead with God. In one swift motion, I flipped on the lights to an empty room. Well, empty except for me and Casey...

'I swear there is someone in here!' she exclaimed.

I checked the door; it was locked. I looked in the closets, under the sink, and under the bed. There was nothing, no one. Finally, after an hour or so, Casey agreed to go back to sleep but only if we left the lights on.

"While I never saw anything, this occurred four more times that fall semester. Each time it happened she was terrified, and each time there was no sign of anyone. Casey swore it was a man– that he was large with wide shoulders.

"Though I never saw him, her description and sightings always made the hair on the back of my neck stand on end.

"After Christmas break, Casey moved out and I filed to have my room become a private one. I would sometimes think of the things that used to happen in the night when Casey lived with me, but I shrugged them off as Casey's bad dreams.

"That was until one warm and bright spring day when something happened I'll never forget...

"I would often go back to my room to nap during the day between classes. Living alone allowed me that type of freedom.

"On this particular day, I was extremely tired. I went to sleep almost as soon as my head hit the pillow. I was just drifting off to a deep sleep, however, when I was suddenly awakened by the unexpected jerk of my ankle being pulled!

"As my leg was tugged so hard I was pulled down in the bed, I could feel icy fingers gripping my ankle. I whipped around, expecting to see my boyfriend there playing a prank on me.

"There was no one there.

"The room was bright with sunlight from the large window and there was no one in sight. I was completely alone.

"I leaped from my bed, thinking the culprit had fled into the hallway, but when I went to open the door I discovered the dead bolt was locked.

"Naturally, I thought of the man Casey had claimed to see all those times. I continued to live in that room for two more years and never saw or felt anything else, but something was there– if only for a moment."

PEARL BUCHANAN THEATRE

WHAT'S A GOOD theater without a ghost?

Attached to the Keene Johnson Building, the Pearl Buchanan Theatre is small and intimate and if you didn't know it was there, you might miss it altogether.

It's also haunted, of course.

The ghost that haunts the theater is the "Blue Lady" and she might just be the most famous ghost on campus. There are certainly more stories about her than any other ghost.

The Blue Lady appears to be a benign spirit who simply enjoys hanging around backstage and up in the loft area above the stage which is used mostly for storage. Everyone from students rehearsing for plays to maintenance men doing work on the building have reported seeing her at one time or another.

AMANDA'S STORY

Amanda was taking a history class and for their final they had to pair up and do a presentation on a topic about the Civil War. The presentations would be given at the Pearl Buchanan Theatre. Neither one of them enjoyed speaking in front of a crowd so Amanda and her partner, Jenny, decided to go in the day before and practice on the stage. They hoped it would help them be more comfortable when they gave their presentation the next day.

Amanda didn't consider herself to be one who easily spooked. She didn't necessarily believe in ghosts and always figured that there was a rational explanation for most things. She'd heard about the "Blue Lady" but didn't know anyone who'd actually seen her.

Arriving at the theater a few minutes early, Amanda went ahead and set up her part of the presentation on stage and, while she waited for her partner, went for a look around. She loved the old theater and thought it had a lot of character. Suddenly, however, in the midst of her exploration, she heard a noise above her. It was a loud crash and sounded like someone had fallen.

Her first thought was that a couple had sneaked in and were having a bit of fun in the empty room. When she didn't hear anything else, though, she grew worried. She didn't think it was a ghost but worried that it might be someone up to no good, and she WAS a woman alone in a building. She wanted to go upstairs and check things out, but common sense told her it wasn't a good idea.

As she stood there, frozen on the stage, the most peculiar thing began to happen. Another thump came from above, but this time, it sounded as though it might be on the top stair. Then, without any warning, the outline of a woman in a light blue dress appeared gliding down the staircase. She was only there for a moment, but Amanda had no doubt in her mind as to what she had seen.

J.D.'S STORY

"J.D." sent in a story about his experience in the theatre via my Haunted Estill County page. I have left the tale in his own words.

"I was in the Pearl Buchanan Theater one night for some Wesley Foundation event and I had been upset over something that had happened earlier in the day so I was slightly agitated. I kept feeling something in there bearing down on me, if that makes any sense. Something magnifying anger in me for no reason, and it made me real nervous, like something was "willing" me to go off on everyone.

"I kept trying to ignore it until one of my friends were goofing off and pinched my butt. They'd sometimes do it, just to be stupid, but this time it set me off for some reason. I jumped up and screamed at him and sat back down. His girlfriend, who was sitting in front of me, asked if I was ok. I couldn't even look her in the eyes and just shook my head no.

"I got up and left, because it felt like the room was suffocating me and I was afraid if someone said something wrong to me I would punch them. I walked around campus for about 2 hours or so trying to cool off. When I got back to the dorm room my friends were worried; they said they didn't even notice me get up and then I was just gone.

"I knew the stories about that theater so I was a little nervous about it in the first place, but something was definitely there amplifying the anger I was already feeling, so much that I *knew* it was external."

WHO IS THE BLUE LADY?

Nobody is really sure *who* the Blue Lady is, how she died, or what she wants, but that doesn't stop the stories from pouring in.

Some students and professors have reported seeing a woman on the stage and in the audience with a faint blue glow emanating from her. The theatre is known for having multiple cold spots and those who are in there late at night or working alone often report feeling as though they're being watched. Visitors have also heard her singing and playing the piano. The voice has been described as "tinged with sadness" and "beautiful" yet also "faintly distant, as though coming from another dimension."

Keith Johnson, an associate professor in the English and theatre department, says that students have often "reported strange sounds and occurrences in the Keen Johnson Building" (Haney, Eastern Progress, 2003). He told the Eastern Progress that students have been reporting "bizarre happenings such as a blue light glowing in the corner of the room or tools being moved with no explanation" since his time with the University in the 1960s and 1970s.

Johnson, himself, has had unusual experiences in the theater. "I experienced it getting cold in the theatre and then it would go away as quickly as it came," Johnson said (Haney, Eastern Progress, 2003). He didn't seem to be frightened, though, and indeed stated that other students thought it was "great fun to have the Blue Lady around."

One popular theory is that she was a theatre student and accidentally hung herself when she went up to the bell tower to practice her lines. Another version of that story is that the hanging was not "accidental" but rather intentional; she was in love with a fellow student who didn't return the feelings. A third version has her performing in a Greek tragedy and under pressure from rehearsing for the performance; her suicide was due to the mounting stress.

Some believe that she was on her way to a performance at the small theatre and died in an accident. Now she haunts the auditorium, trying to put on the performance she never got the chance to in life. Of course, there is an alternate to that tale as well: she *did* perform in the play but died in a train crash on her way back to her parents' town after the performance.

BOONE TAVERN

BOONE TAVERN IS NOT ONLY one of the most haunted places in Madison County, but one of the most haunted hotels in the south. In fact, Patti Starr often hosts a "ghost hunting" weekend at the hotel in which guests can go on their own paranormal adventures in hopes of seeing supernatural spectres.

Several local paranormal groups have hosted investigations at the hotel and restaurant and returned with interesting results. Some have come back with images of shadow people, strange lights, and orbs with their digital cameras. One group set up a camera in one of the hotel rooms and photo-documented an orb traveling from one bed to another.

Some groups have also returned with interesting EVPs from numerous spirits. These tapes have recorded spirits answering direct questions from the investigators, leading investigators to believe that at least some of the spirits are capable of communication.

Various "people" have been spotted throughout the hotel, including a little boy who plays with a ball, a woman in a maid's uniform, and a tall shadow man. Guests have taken pictures that revealed what appeared to be a scared African American boy. Some guests have been awakened in the middle of the night by shaking beds and voices in their rooms.

Of course, there are quite a few stories about the hotel building itself and what may, or may not, have happened there. One story is that the basement was used as a morgue for TB patients at one time. The hotel supposedly created this improvised morgue because the hospital ran out of room.

There is also a rumor that the hotel was part of the Underground Railroad. Of course, the hotel was constructed after the end of the Civil War which makes this highly unlikely. Thanks to some of the rumors about underground tunnels that extend beneath the college's campus, and the sight of an African American boy ghost who occasionally makes his appearance known at the hotel, the rumor about the UR continues to be fueled.

Patti Starr, of Ghost Chasers International Inc., who organizes the ghost hunting weekends, says the hauntings are "nothing to be alarmed about" (Robinson, *Richmond Register*, 2012).

She claims that the spirits are usually "shy" and can even be helpful to us in some situations. In the ghost hunting weekends at Bone Tavern, Starr teaches others how to and where to look for spirits and what equipment is most useful. She insists that the hotel is, indeed, haunted and calls it "a train station with spirits coming and going." She also says that the property has more than one vortex on it.

The majority of the supernatural energy, at least according to the ghost hunters, is in the basement, although there has also been activity spotted on the first and second floors. During one of the ghost hunting weekends, one leader used a short-wave radio to locate a vortex and contact a spirit with it. When Starr asked if there were any spirits there, a voice replied, "Hey" and then later replied that they were "quite a bit" happy when asked if they were satisfied with life on the other side.

BEREA TALES

BEREA'S HISTORY MAY not be long in the grand scheme of things, but it's certainly interesting. Much its past is wound up in the history of Berea College, one of the top liberal arts schools in the south. Berea draws a mix of people seeking a high-quality education, rural way of life, and "artsy" vibe in a small-town setting.

But is it haunted?

It sure looks like it! In this chapter, we'll take a look at some of the haunted locations that don't quite fit in anywhere else.

MORAN SUMMIT ROAD

Berea College might have become famous for its progressive mindset and classrooms, but the area wasn't always so enlightened. Some people believe that numerous slaves were hanged on a bridge on Moran Summit Road. To this day, if you are out there on just the right now, you can still hear the cries of the men and women as they fell to their unjust deaths.

It's not just the sounds of the slaves on the "hanging bridge", however, that people have heard that makes that spot of the road creepy. A mysterious blue light has appeared on multiple occasions as well.

In asking for stories about Berea, "Lily" told me that she had visited the "hanging" bridge on multiple occasions.

"I never get a good feeling there after dark," she said. "It's not just that it's scary because it is that, it's that it's just so sad. If I get out of the car and walk around and let myself feel the place I just want to break down and cry."

She says that she's heard someone crying on more than one occasion and once heard someone screaming "like they were in terrible pain."

"George" who lives near Moran Summit Road, agrees.

"I've been all over that road at all hours of the day and night, and I've never felt good there. It's not so bad in the daytime but sometimes at night, driving along; I could swear that I saw a white light floating around. Just kind of bobbing, like it, was looking for something. And once I heard some woman yelling out a man's name. She just kept hollering and hollering. I had my window rolled down and it sounded like the voice was right there by me. She sounded, I don't know, scared and maybe a little sad."

JEFFERSON STREET RAILROAD CROSSING

According to more than one person I interviewed, a man was struck and killed by a train at the Jefferson Street crossing. His ghost continues to haunt that crossing even today.

The story has become somewhat of a local urban legend, much like that of the ghostly hitchhiker. Supposedly, if you go to the crossing at midnight and call out for the man, he will appear before you, and you can still see him walking down the tracks.

FLAT GAP CHURCH

Another allegedly haunted location is Flat Gap Church. Nobody is sure why the church and surrounding grounds are haunted, but people have been known to hear the sounds of a young woman crying and asking for help. Some say they've seen a little girl wandering around, wearing a bloody dress. Others who have gone out there with recorders and cameras have picked up singing, voices, and pictures of what looks like an angel with expansive wings.

US 25 HOUSE

Since someone is currently residing in it, I am unable to give the exact location of the haunted house on US 25, but several people told me about the rental house that has kept renters awake on more than one occasion.

One gentleman, who asked to be called "Ron," said he lived there with his wife and young son. Not long after moving in, Ron's son began talking to an imaginary friend. Neither parent thought anything about it, at first, but as time went on their son began sharing more and more details about his "friend"–details that seemed much too specific for a four-year-old.

While doing research on the house, I discovered another family who lived in the house for a little while. They were constantly hearing footsteps from people who weren't there, having doors slam in the middle of the night, and waking up to find that things had mysteriously moved around in the house while they slept.

THE COWBELL CEMETERY

Madison County is home to several beautiful, and some creepy, cemeteries. The Salem Cemetery up on Poosey Ridge is probably the most well-known haunted cemetery in the county, but it's not the only one known for being spooky.

The Cowbell Cemetery, located outside of Berea, takes some work getting to since it requires climbing over a fence and walking the rest of the way. Visitors who take the time and effort to reach it, however, are often met with unusual sights: old, homemade headstones and interesting personal items left behind on the graves.

The small cemetery, nestled into the hillside, has around 55 graves. It's not unusual for cemeteries to have an array of personal items and memorabilia placed lovingly on headstones and plots. Cowbell Cemetery, however, seems to have more than its fair share. One of the most unusual things that visitors have captured on film are dolls encased in plastic jugs, glass jars, and other protective cases.

If you're not into the gravesite memorabilia, then you might also find some of the sunken graves fascinating.

CONSPIRACY THEORY

According to some conspiracy theory websites (including Above Top Secret), there are some strange things going on in Berea that might involve aliens, the CIA, the Masons, and the Illuminati (perhaps not all at the same time, but still...)

Some people believe that Berea Community School was built to look like a spaceship because it's a symbol for the fact that aliens are, in fact, living nearby and occasionally host intergalactic meetings.

On the *Above Top Secret* website, a poster on Feb, 7 2007 wrote that he had nearly three rolls of film full of pictures of symbols he had taken around Berea. The symbols supposedly include pentagrams, pentacles, all-seeing eyes, obelisks, and ancient symbols depicting Venus.

THE "COW" STORY

It's not a ghost story from Berea, but it's certainly an interesting one.

A young man actually walked one-hundred miles from his home in the mountains all the way to Berea College. Why? To lead a cow so that he could sell the milk to pay his way through school.

Lots of people were apparently inspired by the boy's motivation and dedication where his education was concerned. Berea's former president, William Goodell Frost, even had pamphlets containing the story printed and distributed for fundraising purposes.

So is this true or an urban legend?

It's actually true, although the real story involved not just one boy but, at least, three. The college has records of more than one individual paying their way through school using a cow or other livestock. The Dean of Berea from 1944-1969 said he knew of at least three boys who drove cows from Eastern Kentucky to sell them for their education expenses. In 1958, an article from the Berea Alumnus reported that Hezekiah Washborn, college student, brought his cow to the college. An additional report claimed that a student named Joshua Flannery paid for his education at Berea through the "cow method" as well.

Then there was Blevins P. Allen. Allen, born in Clay County in 1878, was one of seven children. He paid for his room, board, and fees at Berea with his milk cow. After he had graduated from the grammar school, he continued at Berea to earn a B.L. from the College in 1905.

Berea College President Frost spoke at Allen's mother's funeral in Berea. He cited her as an exemplary "mountain" mother.

At any rate, paying by "cow" is certainly a better deal than racking pu the student loans of today.

BEREA COLLEGE

Like EKU, Berea College has some of its own scholastic ghosts...For instance, a former football player who supposedly died during a game of a broken neck runs up and down the fourth floor of Pearson's Residence Hall. (Burton, *Richmond Register*, 2010).

On October 31st, 2010, *The Richmond Register* published an article entitled "Colleges are favorite 'haunt' for some" and also reported of the ghost of a girl who was raped and subsequently hung herself in an elevator shaft of the James Residence Hall. You can sometimes see her wet footprints.

The same issue mentioned "eerie candles, and the creaking of a rocking chair in the attic of Fairchild Residence Hall" which are supposedly the "spirit of a girl who hung herself in the attic sometime in the 1800s, after she had discovered she was pregnant and was spurned by her boyfriend." (This morality tale is a fairly common urban legend that can be found on college campuses throughout the United States.)

Then there is the ghost story involving the ghost of Opal Sturgell. Opal is said to haunt the grounds of the college campus and has been doing so since her death in 1937. Sadly, she was shot and murdered by her ex-boyfriend, George Elmo Wells, in 1937.

Opal and George had attended high school together. He'd proposed back then but she'd declined. Once they entered college at Berea, he pursued her but she was apparently not interested since several people, including the dean, had told him to stay away from her. His grades began to suffer and it's obvious he was having some issues going on inside.

On 15, August 1937 Opal was outside of Phelps Stokes Chapel with fellow student William Anderson. Wells approached the couple, asked if he could speak with Opal, and she told him she wouldn't leave Anderson. When she refused to leave with him, Wells replied, "If that's the way you feel about it, okay - you may be sorry" and then left. However, as Sturgell and Anderson began to walk away, as they were nearing Lincoln Hall, Wells reportedly jumped out at them from behind a bush. He attacked Opal and grabbed her and then shot her when Anderson tried to help. Wells ended up shooting her two more times. Anderson said that Sturgell attempted to whisper something to him after he shot Opal, but Anderson couldn't hear what he was saying. He also never got served justice, since he took off after the killing and was never seen again, in spite of police efforts and years of searching.

During the murder investigation, police found a poem inside Wells' room, believed to have been written by him about Opal. It reads as follows:

To A Lady

Where flowers bloom along the road of life
The weary traveler breathes their fragrance sweet,
and thus forgets his daily toil and strife,
Engulfed in that which could make life complete
All petals hold within their form so clear,
A beauty which the open eyes may see,
and find that they in all their glory
Are reflections of the great reality.

Thou are a flower blooming in the spring
Whose loveliness is glorious divine.
Thy radiant glow and cheerful smiles may bring
To someone happiness and joy sublime
And courage great to help him to be true

Along the path made beautiful by you

(Read more about this tragedy at the Berea archives' website: http://libraryguides.berea.edu/murdersoncampus. Written by K. Olivia Meszaros, Last Updated: Dec 8, 2015 4:19 AM)

Lastly, there is an organ in Presser Music Hall which will "begin to play by itself."

OTHER HAUNTED HOUSES

IN DOING RESEARCH for this book I came across several other references to haunted houses in Madison County, most of them privately owned. ..

There is a house located in downtown Richmond that was once used as a funeral home. For the past thirty years it's been a private residence but, up until fairly recently, still had the big green awning out front that signified its former use.

I've encountered numerous people that either lived in that house (mostly college students) or passed through it at one time or another and swear it's haunted.

And not haunted by anything friendly.

"The house is possessed," one former resident claimed. "It needs a priest to go through it."

Another former resident said that in addition to the whispering voices that could be heard in the halls, the heavy footsteps, and the items that would move from one room to another on their own, a "growling" noise could also be heard on occasion.

BARNES MILL ROAD

There is a white house with maroon shutters on Barnes Mill Road. It was once a private home but has since been turned into apartments. It's also been deserted several times over the years.

One former resident writes on Topix.com about an experience they had there:

"I used to live there and some really crazy stuff happened there. My daughter just felt this compulsion to look inside the air condition vent in her room and (don't ask me why because I never could figure out why she wanted to look in it). When she finally got the grate off of it she found an old brown paper bag stuffed way in the back of it. When she tried to open it, it just fell apart in her hands because it was so old it was brittle. Inside the bag was human hair. We started freaking out. The screwdriver she used to remove the grate was laid on the kitchen table. It was a Craftsman screwdriver and it flew off my kitchen table and snapped in half. Solid steel does not snap in half just by falling on the floor. Needless to say, we moved very soon after that. Not long after we moved out, a two-year-old little girl was murdered in the apartment downstairs from the one we lived in."

In addition to that story, I spoke to another former resident who lived in the house for a little over a year. They told me that one night they were home alone, waiting for their wife to get home from work. It was getting late, but they didn't like going to bed alone. He ended up making himself some popcorn and watching television on the couch. He said he must have dozed off because the next thing he knew, he heard the front door opening. He opened his eyes and could hear someone walking towards the couch. He then felt icy fingertips on the back of his neck.

"I started to make a joke about her hands being cold and how I was going to get her back for scaring me like that," he said, "but when I turned around, there was nobody there."

He thought perhaps he was dreaming but when he felt the nape of his neck, it was ice-cold. Shaken, he jumped from the couch and turned around. The front door was standing wide open. As he stood there studying the door, his wife's car drove up.

The former resident who posted on Topix.com stated that they thought "That place should be burned to the ground."

LOCUST AVENUE

On the *Ghosts of America* website, "Ronda" offers a story about a house she lived in on Locust Avenue.

Ronda insists that the house had a "darkness" in it and that it caused a variety of problems while her family was living there. First, she says, there was "arguing all the time." After some time, she became depressed, and her husband started showing signs of violence, where violent tendencies had never been apparent in him before.

In addition to the personal problems she and her husband were experiencing, there were also signs of what sounds like poltergeist activity in the house: lamps broke, something jumped on Ronda's bed while she was in it, and voices in the night would call out to the residents.

Things apparently got worse for Ronda when she was home alone. Her depression worsened, and she even began having suicidal thoughts. As she slept, the paranormal activity would get worse. She could feel the presence in the house, even as she slept, and ignoring it was not an option—that caused the spirit to get angry, and it would retaliate by knocking things off the wall. Sometimes it even shook her.

Ronda eventually left the house with her child and things began looking up for her almost immediately.

WESTOVER AVENUE

We lived in and owned a house on Westover Avenue for many years. Just a few houses down from Main Street, the brick house is unassuming from the outside. Several visitors over the years, however, left us convinced our house was haunted.

When we first moved in, I invited a friend over. She claimed to have some psychic abilities and asked if she could walk through the house; she claimed she could feel some supernatural stuff going on. I said sure.

I had felt a few strange things in the house, too, but didn't tell her any of the experiences I'd had. I wanted to see what she'd say first.

After walking through the house and she came back downstairs and found me. "The little room off your bedroom?" she asked. "There is a ton of sadness in it. I felt the most energy there. Like maybe someone used to just go in there and cry their eyes out."

I also had trouble with that room and couldn't sleep if the door was open. I'd always felt like someone was watching me. When I slept in the room across the hall, I would regularly wake up and catch a glimpse of someone walking down the short hallway between the rooms, too.

Years later, I had another friend come and stay. She'd been there two nights and was looking poorly. When I asked what was wrong, she said she'd been unable to sleep—that our house was haunted and the ghosts were keeping her up at night. I told her she could sleep with me that night. My mother had the larger bed, so Cece and I slept in that room and put my mom in my bed.

At some point in the middle of the night, there was a loud crashing noise. I woke up and, blurry from sleep, for a brief second caught the unmistakable sight of a woman in a long white dress standing at the end of our bed, at my feet.

I jumped up, threw on the light, and looked at Cece (who was awake). "Did you see anything?" I asked her.

"You mean the woman in the white dress by the bed?" she asked. "She's here every night."

My mother came running into the room at that point. (She, by the way, was wearing red.) Her bed had broken; that was the crash we'd heard.

I wanted to talk to the ghost and find out who she was but as I began speaking aloud, Cece begged me to stop. She said others would come and that the breaking bed had been a "warning."

MOUNT VERNON ROAD

Another contributor on Ghosts of America shared a story about their time in a house in Berea.

The contributor, who identifies themselves as "Charlie" states that he lived in a house in which he had "multiple bad experiences." These included objects flying around the room by themselves. Doors were known to open and close by themselves and at times the residents would wake up to the sight of a little girl staring back and giggling. They also spotted a "tall man in a hat" standing behind them in the bathroom mirror.

THE BRECK HOUSE

The Breck House, located on Lancaster Avenue, is another house that is reportedly haunted. This time, the house is haunted by a man who was murdered in the front yard.

In 1887, Nannette Harris, daughter of Richmond physician, Dr. John M. Harris, married G. W. Willis. Nannette's family, including her brother Robert, was not happy about the marriage, which is probably why she eloped. The couple moved into the Judge C.H. Breck house. On April 8, 1887, Robert Harris met Willis at the property. They soon began arguing. Onlookers heard Harris tell Willis that if he had had a pistol, he would have killed him. Harris then apparently made the fatal mistake of reaching into his pocket. Willis then got out his own pistol and open-fired on Harris. Harris died several days later, but Willis was found having acted in self-defense, especially since investigators produced a pistol from Harris' pocket.

One guest who stayed at the Breck House many years ago told me that in the middle of the afternoon, at approximately the same time Harris was killed, she was sure she'd heard a gunshot ring out from the yard. A neighbor verified the gun shot sound and said he'd heard similar things coming from the property and has never been able to explain it.

SLAVE HOUSES

Former residents of a house on Curtis Pike talk about hearing "chanting, singing, and talking" from the remains of the slave cabins that are in the backyard. They said that they mostly heard the noises at night, and more frequently in the fall than any other time of the year.

"One time we were having a party," the former resident said, "and a bunch of us were sitting outside in the yard. It was starting to get dark and things were winding down. We'd been going all afternoon. All of a sudden we all heard this singing. There must have been half a dozen voices, all singing together."

She went on to say that at first they thought the noise was echoing from someplace else but then they realized it was coming from where the slave cabins were.

"We walked down there a little ways, there were five of us in all, and listened. The singing got fainter as we got closer but you could still hear it. It was definitely there."

SALEM CEMETERY

FOR MOST OF my life, I've heard about the Salem Cemetery, up on Poosey Ridge, and the ghosts that haunt it.

There are the floating orbs investigators have captured on film, the red eyes that appear to "float" over certain graves at night, and the distinctive howling that can be heard that doesn't sound as though it belongs to anything human.

"It's a ghost that haunts it."

"There's a demon that lives there."

"A witch cursed it."

"It's the site of an old Indian burial ground."

"They hung a witch there."

The stories about this picturesque, unassuming looking cemetery are countless. But is it haunted?

This one, unfortunately for me, remains a mystery.

THE GYPSY DEATH

THIS IS NOT a ghost story but it *is* a story about a death and is so intriguing that it was impossible not to share it here at the end.

If you would like to read the whole story, visit:

The Strange Funeral Here in 1935 http://library-old.eku.edu/blogs/digital/items/show/1393

In April of 1935, a caravan of more than forty "gypsies" stopped north of Richmond on Lexington Road. Tom Mitchell, the group's leader, crossed the road to the Deatherage service station trying to find somewhere to camp for the night. A few minutes later, a truck loaded with 11,000 pounds of flour struck one of the cars in the gypsy caravan and then sideswiped three of the others. Tom and his brother were killed, and a child was also injured.

When the gypsies at the hospital discovered their leader had died, they took out candles and placed them all over the room then started marching around and chanting.

They established a temporary a camp on Four Mile Road and became somewhat of a local spectacle. A lot of them went barefooted and dressed in strange clothes. After a new leader had been chosen, they continued their mourning.

During the funeral many other gypsies came for the ritual after hearing about the tragedy in local papers. They all gathered in the Richmond Cemetery at the double grave. Father Oscar Poole of St. Mark's Roman Catholic Church blessed the grave and then something really strange happened: The two coffins were opened, and the dead men's father got between his sons and placed an arm over each one. Overwhelmed with grief, he then starting beating his fists upon his head.

The two bodies were buried with hats, shoes, a comb, a mirror, soap, and cigarettes. Members of the tribe dropped in coins as they marched by. Unfortunately, the amount was greatly exaggerated which caused grave robbers to try to dig the poor men up later on.

LILLIAN BAINS KARNES

ONE OF THE BEST ghost stories I've heard about Madison County never happened. It's not untrue in the sense that the person just made it up–it's untrue in the sense that the person who made it up was so dedicated to their job that they actually managed to convince lots of people online that the story and history were true.

Meet Lillian Karnes, aka Lillian Bains.

The "story" started out like this...

"The most haunted place in this county has to be the old Baines orphanage. Not only did all those kids disappear, but the people that checked it out got gone as well. My Mom told us as kids to stay away from there because the people that went out there vanished and all that was found were their eyes."

Lillian lived in a house that is now somewhere on the Depot's grounds. It was an orphanage for awhile, until she killed some of the children. Lillian was a terrible person. She killed people, including the kids in her care. She buried their body parts all over the place. She cursed and hexed people. She, herself, was finally murdered.

Her house, still standing, is not only haunted–it's evil. Depot people won't go near it. People have gone blind from entering it, have gone crazy, have had horrible things happen to them just from working around it...

And her spirit might just follow you home, where other horrible fates might befall you.

The Depot workers are all sworn to refute the tale and even lie about the house's existence. It's been removed from the archives of local history sources. Older generations remember Lillian, of course.

And none of this happened. None of it. It was all in the imagination of a person on Topix who decided to make up their own story under a thread about local haunted houses.

He/she was so convincing about this story, even creating multiple accounts and signing in and commenting on her own threads to back herself up, that there were people bringing up Google Earth and maps and trying to find the house. People "remembered" their grandparents talking about the story. People Googled Lillian and found references to what they "thought" might have been her.

This went on for several months.

It was one of the best ghost stories I've ever read.

Too bad it wasn't true.

ADDITIONAL PHOTOS

The following are some pictures I've taken while interviewing folks, investigating different parts of the county, and going for drives. These aren't necessarily "haunted," just older homes and maybe a little forgotten...

SPECIAL THANKS

THERE ARE LOTS of people who were responsible for helping make this book possible.

First, I'd like to thank my husband, EKU professor Peter Howard. He helped in MANY ways, including taking a lot of the pictures for the book.

My son, 8-year-old Sam, was helpful as well. He went with me on some of the interviews and is always my sounding board for the stories. He listens intently while I read them aloud to him and then truthfully tells me whether or not he finds them "creepy."

Suzie Ratliff, high school AND adult friend, graciously shared her memories with me.

Lots of people on my Haunted Estill County page pulled through and submitted stories to me to use for the book. I enjoyed reading them and tried to use as many as I could.

Lastly, I have to thank my mother. Before I had my license, she was the one driving me around the county as a young teenager, helping me find the haunted places and old, mysterious houses and going on my first "adventures" with me.

I will never be able to repay all the gas and snack money she spent on these outings. And she is still finding places to go, posting them regularly on my FB page and asking if it looks like something worth "checking out."

Thanks, Mom.

REFERENCES

Unusual Kentucky Blog. *UFO Blitz in the Bluegrass Triangle.* MARCH 30, 2011. <http://unusualkentucky.blogspot.com/2011/03/ufo-blitz-in-bluegrass-triangle.html>

K. Olivia Meszaros, *Murders on Campus.* Last Updated: Dec 8, 2015 4:19 AM. <http://libraryguides.berea.edu/murdersoncampus>

McQueen, Keven. *Murder in Old* Kentucky. McClanahan Publishing House; First Edition edition (July 1, 2005).

Unusual Kentucky Blog. *Tunnels Under Richmond.* APRIL 28, 2008. <http://unusualkentucky.blogspot.com/2008/04/tunnels-under-richmond.html>

The Cincinnati Enquirer, September 21, 1936. Page 1. <http://cincinnati.newspapers.com/newspage/100143888/>

Dr. Robert Grise, "Strange Funeral Here in 1935," *Madison's Heritage Online*, accessed October 9, 2015, <http://library-old.eku.edu/blogs/digital/items/show/1393>

Robinson, Bill. *The Richmond Register*. "Ghost hunters detect spirits at Boone Tavern." Apr 2, 2012. <http://www.richmondregister.com/localnews/x1451003061/Ghost-hunters-detect-spirits-at-Boone-Tavern#sthash.aLhAEB02.dpuf>

Haynes, Brittney. *The Eastern Progress*. "EKU Ghosts." October 27, 2005.

Bender, Keila. Bit of the Bluegrass. "Ghosts of EKU." June 7, 2014. <http://www.bitofthebluegrass.com/2010/10/ghosts-of-eku.html>

Haney, Tracy. *The Eastern Progress*. "The Haunting of The Blue Lady and other Eastern spirits." October 30, 2003.
<http://www.easternprogress.com/2003/10/30/the-haunting-of-the-blue-lady-and-other-eastern-spiritsbr/>

McQueen, Keven. *Cassius M. Clay*. Jun 16, 2001. Turner Publishing.

Burton, Emily. *Richmond Register*. "Colleges are favorite 'haunt' for some." October 31, 2010.
<http://www.richmondregister.com/localnews/x1507929641/Colleges-are-favorite-haunt-for-some/print>

National UFO Reporting Center. State Report Index For KY.
<http://www.nuforc.org/webreports/ndxlky.html>

Kentucky Bigfoot.
<http://www.kentuckybigfoot.com/7_5_08_thru_2_11_09.htm>

Unusual Kentucky Blog. The Blue Grass Army Depot. OCTOBER 24, 2008. <http://unusualkentucky.blogspot.com/2008/10/blue-grass-army-depot.html>

Barnes Mill House: Topix.com <http://www.topix.com/forum/city/richmond-ky/TO8UVEFHS63NHNPQE>

Little Egypt: Topix.com <http://www.topix.com/forum/city/richmond-ky/TO8UVEFHS63NHNPQE>

Unusual Kentucky Blog. *Madison Middle School.* July 10, 2008. <http://unusualkentucky.blogspot.com/2008/07/madison-middle-school-ghost-photo.html>

Ghosts of America. *Richmond, Kentucky Ghost Sightings.* <http://www.ghostsofamerica.com/4/Kentucky_Richmond_ghost_sightings.html>

Ghosts of America. *Berea, Kentucky.* <http://www.ghostsofamerica.com/4/Kentucky_Berea_ghost_sightings.html>

Unusual Kentucky Blog. *Pigg House of Berea.* June 9, 2008. <http://unusualkentucky.blogspot.com/2008/06/pigg-house-of-berea.html>

Unusual Kentucky Blog. *Black Helicopters in Kentucky.* October 21, 2008. <http://unusualkentucky.blogspot.com/2008/10/black-helicopters-in-kentucky.html>

Unexplained Mysteries. "Pigg House." 06 December 2005 - 06:08 AM. Posted by "Mr. E." <http://www.unexplained-mysteries.com/forum/index.php?showtopic=51205&st=30>

Cornett, Kaylia. *The Eastern Progress.* "Real Haunted Places." October 28, 2010. <http://www.easternprogress.com/2010/10/28/real-haunted-placesbr/>

The Crypto Crew. "Ghost caught in photo at Sullivan Hall." October 5, 2012. <http://www.thecryptocrew.com/2012/10/ghost-caught-in-photo-at-sullivan-hall.html>

Lainhart, Taylor. & Ferrell, Whitney. *Upward Bound.* Haunting of Sullivan Hall. July 5, 2012. Volume 1, Issue 2. <http://upwardbound.eku.edu/sites/upwardbound.eku.edu/files/07-05-12.pdf>

Luttress, Bethany & Goode, Megan. Upward Branch. "Keen Johnson Haunting: The Blue Lady." July 12, 2012. Volume 1, Issue 3.

Ghost Eyes: Most Haunted Places in America. *Haunted Schools: Eastern Kentucky University.* September 22, 2012. <http://www.ghosteyes.com/haunted-schools-eastern-kentucky-university>

Dr. Robert Grise, "Hung as a Spy," Madison's Heritage Online, accessed September 1, 2015, <http://library-old.eku.edu/blogs/digital/items/show/1480>

ABOUT THE AUTHOR

Rebecca Patrick-Howard is the author of several books including the paranormal mystery series *Taryn's Camera*. She lives in eastern Kentucky with her husband and two children. Visit her website at:

www.rebeccaphoward.net

LET'S CONNECT

Find Rebecca online and connect through social media.

Pinterest: https://www.pinterest.com/rebeccapatrickh/

Website: www.rebeccaphoward.net

Email: rphwrites@gmail.com

Facebook: https://www.facebook.com/rebeccahowardwrites

Twitter: https://twitter.com/RPHWrites

Instagram: https://instagram.com/rphwrites/

A BROOM WITH A VIEW

Kentucky Witches, Book 1

Rebecca Patrick-Howard

Order NOW

http://www.rebeccaphoward.net/a-broom-with-a-view.html

She's your average witch next door.
He's a Christmas tree farmer with three sisters named after horses.
It's a town so small it doesn't even have a Walmart.
None of them will ever be the same again...

Liza Jane Higginbotham is your average witch next door. Just a down home girl, she enjoys driving her truck, listening to country music and, oh yes, the occasional brew.

This witch just wants to enjoy the quiet life. When her no-good, hipster husband cheats on her with a trombone player, she moves back to take over the family farm in rural Eastern Kentucky. Here, she's expecting some peace, content to play in her garden, restore the dilapidated farmhouse, and throw her money away at the town auction house every Friday night.

But the town of Kudzu Valley just won't let a witch rest. From the high school basketball coach looking for a charm to help the team win the big game to Lola Ellen Pearson who wants to hex the local Pizza Hut for giving her food poisoning the night before her fourth wedding, everyone wants SOMETHING from the town's resident witch!

When Cotton Hashagen's dead body is found, though, all eyes turn to Liza Jane. After all, hadn't she JUST accused the librarian of a terrible crime? With the townspeople and police turning their eyes to Liza Jane, it's going to take a lot for her to prove that she didn't put a "whammy" on him AND solve the mystery to find the real culprit!

OTHER BOOKS

Taryn's Camera Series

Windwood Farm (Book 1)

Griffith Tavern (Book 2)

Dark Hollow Road (Book 3)

Shaker Town (Book 4)

Jekyll Island (Book 5)

Black Raven Inn (Book 6)

Taryn's Pictures: Photos from Taryn's Camera

Kentucky Witches

A Broom with a View

Broommates (Coming Summer 2016)

A Broom of One's Own (Coming Fall 2016)

True Hauntings

Haunted Estill County

More Tales from Haunted Estill County

Haunted Estill County: The Children's Edition

Haunted Madison County

A Summer of Fear

The Maple House

Four Months of Terror

Two Weeks: A True Haunting

Three True Tales of Terror

Other Books

Coping with Grief: The Anti-Guide to Infant Loss

Three Minus Zero

Finding Henry: A Journey Into Eastern Europe

Estill County in Photos

Haunted: Ghost Children Stories From Beyond

Haunted: Houses